APPLY THE LAWS IN THIS SERIES AND EXPERIENCE

TRANSFIGURATION

Sister Thedra

Volume VIII of VIII

INCLUDES

"THE HOUSE OF THE LORD"

ISBN: 978-1-7373071-4-3

TRANSFIGURATION

A complete change of form or appearance into a more beautiful or spiritual state. "in this light the junk undergoes a transfiguration; it shines"

The transfiguration is a sign that Jesus was to fulfill the Law and the prophets. It also assured James, Peter, and John that Jesus was indeed the Messiah.

In Christian teachings, the Transfiguration is a pivotal moment, and the setting on the mountain is presented as the point where human nature meets God: the meeting place for the temporal and the eternal, with Jesus himself as the connecting point, acting as the bridge between heaven and earth.

To the Reader

Please read and review "Divine Explanations" on page 224 for questions and definitions of terms.

This book is only a portion of the teachings and prophecies that have been given by Sananda (Jesus Christ), Sanat Kumara, and others of the higher realms, and Recorded by Sister Thedra.

Dedication

These volumes, entitled TRANSFIGURATION are dedicated to Sheryl McCartney and Kamalakar Durgapu, without whose invaluable assistance this work would not have been possible.

Contents

Esu Jesus Sananda

This reproduction is from an actual photograph taken on June 1st, 1961, in Chichen Itza, Yucatan, by one of thirty archaeologists working in the area at the time. Sananda appeared in visible, tangible body and permitted His photograph to be taken.

THE REWARD

Sori Sori --Hear ye me - and record that which I say unto thee - for it shall go into the Book of Life - for them which shall follow in the way of Light and resurrection ---

I say unto thee - discount not mine words - for they are Holy - and they shall be remembered by them which have gone the way of Light.

I say unto thee: These words shall stand as mine testimony unto thee for all time - for the age of revelation is now come - and man shall know that which goes on in the realms of Light ---

He as of this age hast walked blindly - yet now he shall awaken - and know for a surety that he is not alone - that he is one with the "ALL"- and there is no separation save his unknowing - his own blindness -- Yet I am come that he might be made to see - - so let it be as the Father hast willed it ---

For there is the Host and the Council - and there is the Father which stand ever ready to reveal the "Word" - the "Work" unto all which are prepared to receive - and none shall be denied -- Let it suffice that I am come that they be found and sorted - that they be put into their proper place - that they be brot out of their darkness - as they are prepared - "as they are prepared so shall they receive"- so be it the law ---

While it is recorded that there is but one Lord God - there is the Mighty Host which stands by to assist in their ascent - and for this have they been prepared ---

Now - I say unto thee mine beloved: Ye shall be as one prepared to give assistance unto others in like manner -- Ye shall be as one brot into the place wherein I am - and ye shall receive from me thy enua - and ye shall stand as one prepared to go into all the lands of the Earth - and find them which cry out for assistance -- Ye shall call forth and I shall give unto thee the assistance which is necessary unto that which is given unto thee to do - for ye shall not fail - ye shall not want - neither shall ye call in vain - for ye shall be answered ---

Ye shall be as one blest - for I shall give unto thee of myself that ye be blest -- So be it and Selah ---

For this day let it be said - that one shall come unto thee and he shall give unto thee a part - and he shall be as one on whose head I have placed mine hand - and he walks with me and he is as one prepared to assist thee in that which is at hand ---

Fear not - as it is said many times: I am with thee unto the end - and mine hand I have placed upon thine head in holy benediction - and ye have followed where I have lead thee -- Thou hast proven thyself in all things - now ye shall find thine reward - and it shall be as nothing thou hast known -- I say - thou hast prepared for thyself thine own reward - for thine own reward is thy service rendered -- So be it and Selah ---

Now - I say - thine reward shall be great indeed - for ye shall stand before the throne of the Most High - and receive from Him thine own estate - which hast been held in trust for thee - and ye shall rejoice forevermore-- So be it and Selah -- Praise ye the name of Solen Aum Solen which hast given unto thee Being - for He is the Father - and I am the Son -- Thou art one with the Father-the-Son - and ye shall be as one with Him - and KNOW thou art one with the WHOLE - for this is thine inheritance - willed unto thee from the beginning -- So be it and Selah

Recorded by Sister Thedra

Justice

Sori Sori-- Justice shall reign supreme in all that is done in the House of the Lord - and justice shall be as nothing which man calls "Justice"- for he is not given unto such justice as we know - that which hast been brot about thru the fiat of God the Father ---

Knowing that justice is that which was from the beginning - of Him, of His Nature - of His Mind - for all things were created for to glorify Him - and for His use -- Therefore He gives - and He takes away - He adds to - and subtracts - and for this I say - He works in and thru all things - all beings- be they man or beast ---

When it is come that ye stand upon mine High Holy Mount with me - ye shall see that there is no injustice in all His creation - for even the lion and the lamb shall lay down at His feet as one - and therein shall be no animosity - no hatred - no war between them ---

Now it is come when ye shall be as one sent into the places wherein they war - with themself - and their surroundings - and even their own shadows - which seem so real unto them -- Ye shall be unto them as I am unto thee - ye shall minister unto them - and they shall be as ones which have a mind to receive thine hand - which shall be unto them great comfort and assistance -- So be it and Selah ---

Hast it not been said - that there shall be changes made? - and it is for this that I have called unto thee: "Make ye haste that ye be as one prepared to do that which I do" - for I shall give unto thee a part - and it shall be as none other -- Ye shall go out amongst them which do mourn - and ye shall find them which cry for assistance - and ye shall lay thy hand on them and bless them as I have blest thee - and for this have I prepared thee -- So be it as the Father hast willed it ---

Let thy hand be mine hand - thy feet mine feet - thy words mine words - and ye shall carry mine banner as thy shield - and thy protection shall be thine -- Fear not! Let it be - do as I have said - and it shall be for the good of all mankind -- So be it and Selah --

Amen and Amen --

So be it -- So be it -- So be it --

Recorded by Sister Thedra

Whither Goest Thou?

Sori Sori -- Shall it be the one which hast his hand in mine - or shall it be the one which sets his foot against me - which does the work of the Lord?

Shall it be the one which follows where I lead - or shall it be the one which goes the way of the enemy? I say it shall be the one which follows where I lead him - for him I shall favor - him shall I attend - him shall I give unto in greater measure -- Him shall I lead - and direct that he might go where I go -- So be it I shall bless him which chooses the way I go - for I am he which is sent that they be found and brot out of bondage - freed from their own imprisonment - - for I have said: "All things according unto the law"-- It is the law: As they are prepared so shall they receive -- So be it that I have said: "Choose ye wisely"- and it shall profit thee to follow after me - for it is the strait and sure way. So be it and Selah --

Recorded by Sister Thedra

From Whence Cometh Our Strength

Sori Sori -- This is the hour that I would set aside for this mine communication for <u>this part</u> -- While it is but the second best - I say it is second best -- yet the rest is necessary unto thy body - and it is for this reason that we provide thee sleep ---

When it is come that ye have had sufficient rest - we shall appoint thee another part -- When it is come that sleep is not required - we shall give unto thee another appointment - - - So be it that ye shall now rest the physical vehicle - and it shall be of great value unto thee - So let it serve thee well ---

I am come that ye be prepared for a part which is new unto thee -- So be it and Selah ---

While it is given unto me to know thy strength - I too know thy weakness -- And I have said that I shall strengthen thee in thy weak parts - so be it I shall do mine part ---

While it is given unto <u>me</u> to know thy weakness - I too know mine strength - which shall be strength which shall be thine - and no more shall ye be deficient in strength and power - for I shall endow ye with power <u>and</u> strength which <u>is</u> <u>mine</u> ---

Pay ye heed unto mine word - and give no thot unto them which would take from me one part of mine power - mine word - mine strength - for do they not say - I am all powerful - and is it not mine to give? Wherein have I failed them? Yet they make a mockery of mine words/ mine sayings ---

Wherein have they proven them to be a lie? Have I not given unto them of mine own self that they might have Being? Yet they use that power to torment themself - while in their misery thy ask for deliverance from their own creation ----

Wherein is it given unto me to add unto their misery? I stand by to assist them - to give unto them of mine own self - mine wisdom - mine help - mine strength - that they win their victory over their own pitiful weakness - over their own creation -- Yet they are slow of foot and sluggish of mind - the pity of it - they have not proven me - neither mine word - for it is said: "Prove me"-- I shall do mine part and ye shall do thine - and be ye as one which hast proven me in all things -- So be it ye shall be blest in the doing --

I Am that I AM

Recorded by Sister Thedra

Solen Aum Solen - The Power - Light - Released

Sori Sori -- Be ye as the hand of me made manifest - and record ye that which I say unto thee - for it shall be for the good of all mankind ---

Ye shall give it unto them as it is given unto thee - for no word - not even one letter shall be taken from or added to -- So be it that I am come that they might be prepared for the greater part ---

While it is yet not come that they are prepared - I have prepared a place for them - and they shall be brot forth as ones prepared to enter in ---

When they have prepared themself to enter - then I shall receive them in the name of mine Father Which hast sent me ---

There are many which keep the way of the Lord - there are many which keep watch - and they have prepared themself for their part -- It is said - as ye are prepared so shall ye receive -- So be it and Selah ---

When it is come that ye are prepared - ye shall stand before the Throne of the Most High Living God - and He shall give unto thee that which hast been kept for thee -- He shall place upon thy head a Crown of Living Light - which shall not weigh heavy upon thy head -- Ye shall wear it with dignity and with joy - for it shall be thine by divine inheritance ---

Blest is the one which is crowned by Him - the Giver of Life -- Behold Him ye Sons of God - gather round - and be ye as ones prepared to receive thine inheritance in full -- Praise ye His Name Solen Aum Solen - for He hast given unto thee the Name which ye shall adore - and sing His praise forevermore -- There is power in the Name - use it for the good of all mankind -- Bless thyself - for it is given thee that all be lifted up ---

The time is now come when the Name shall go forth - as the Name of the One and Only Father - Which hast given unto us Being - for each day brings its revelation - Each people has that which is allotted unto them for that day ---

I say - the day is now come when they shall come into greater knowledge - and this is mine part - to place before them such knowledge as shall profit them ---

Now as of old - there are ones which shall deny me - and dispute mine authority - and deny me as of old - the POWER AND AUTHORITY WHICH IS MINE by Divine Rite -- So be it that I am not of a mind to be given the bitter cup - for I shall not drink from their cup again! ---

I say - they shall learn the way of righteousness - by drinking their own cup - they shall drink the portion which they have prepared for me for I say - as ye give so shall ye receive - it is the law ---

Bear ye witness of me - and give heed unto mine words - and I shall reveal unto thee many things - for this is the day of revelation - the day of atonement -- So be it that I come to assist thee in thy ascent - therefore - I say: "Come ye unto me - and I shall give unto thee as thou art prepared to receive" -- So let it be as the Father hast willed it --

Recorded by Sister Thedra

The Green Nut Tree - The Harvest

Sori Sori -- Let this be recorded and let it be given unto them which have prepared themself to receive it - for it shall profit them to hear that which I say unto thee -- So be it that I am come that they might come to know the true from the false ---

There are ones which would receive thee - there are ones which would take from thee thy gift - and leave thee poverty stricken and without favor with me -- Yet I say: Ye shall stand firm and bend not before them - ye shall be as one tried and found worthy - so be it the Will of the Father which hast sent me -- So be it and Selah ---

Now ye shall say unto them in mine name - that there are none which enter into the Holy of Holies unprepared -- Their good works shall be as nought - without cleansing of the "Cup" -- The cup shall first be emptied - cleansed - and I shall fill it to the brim - yea - to overflowing -- It is said that: "They shall drink from the overflow and be satisfied" -- So be it and Selah -- For that matter I say unto thee: It shall be that which overflows from mine cup that fills thine --

And it is said that there is a river which flows from the Throne of God - it is so - and from that river shall I flood thy place - and I shall set up a place wherein ye shall stand - as one prepared to give unto the weary and heavy laden - as I have given unto thee -- I say - ye shall be as one responsible for the part which I give unto thee -- So be it that ye have proven thyself - and I know that which I say - that which I am about -- I say I am not asleep - neither am I afraid to speak out - for I am prepared to prove that which I say -- And that which I do shall be known - and they which sleep shall be as ones asleep - they shall be awakened in due season - and the ones which shall follow me shall find that they have chosen well ---

Now it is come when I shall walk among them - and I shall touch them and they shall respond unto my touch and be as ones come alive. They shall come unto me and rejoice in the knowing that I am come into their midst - for their response shall I too rejoice! ---

While it is said that they shall respond unto mine touch - it is said too - that some shall sleep on - for they are as wont to sleep - they are as the green nut - they are as yet not prepared to come forth -- So let the "sleepers" sleep - and make ye haste - for I say unto thee: each season hast its harvest -- Cry not over the green nut tree - for it shall yield up its harvest in due season -- So be it and Selah ---

Fortune thyself to be one of the few which hast come forth as the first harvest which is prepared to be brot into the place wherein I am - for I say unto thee - thou hast been thru the mill - the furnace - and the refining hast proven thy worth - thy mettle -- So be it that these are mine own words - and I speak fearlessly - and no man shall put his foot into mine mouth - for I am the Lord of Lords - I am come that these things be made known - and none shall deny mine words - or say me nay ---

This hast been mine time and I have used it well -- For the good of all have I spoken - for the good of the few have I said that which they might understand ---

Now ye shall place that which wast shown thee - with this which I now command thee to record - and it too shall be given unto them - for them which have the mind to comprehend -- So be it that they which have the mind to receive shall receive in mine name - and be glad for their gifts - which shall be bestowed upon them in the fashion designed within the Inner Temple -- So be it and Selah

Recorded by Sister Thedra

Sori Sori -- Note that I have said a new work ye shall be given - so be it it is now begun - and ye shall do a mighty work -- So be it and Selah

Sori Sori -- Let this be the time for revelation - the time for knowing and it shall be for the good of All - Hear ye that which I say unto thee, and be ye as one prepared to know -- So be it it shall be revealed - that which is said - let it avail thee much -- Much wisdom shall come from that which is revealed unto thee

In Spirit - Revelation: The Banquet

In spirit I was in a bleak barren city -- all the streets lined with one continuous building on either side - with the same monotonous design and color - or rather - the absence of color - only drabness -- Many doors - indicating many apartments -- I was impressed by the emptiness of the place - the absence of people on the streets -- I had only seen into two places in my wanderings thru the place - - I stood penniless - - did not remember a friend or an address -- I began to inquire for an address from whence I had gone some time ago - - I entered one store and inquired where I might get a pair of shoes -- The keeper showed me a pair of furry slippers - - I said I would not need them - I needed walking shoes -- All the stores dealt in "Coats of skin" - I had no need for such.

I remembered the many times in Earth Cities - when I had given bus fare to stranded strangers - and wondered who might give unto me as I had unto them - - - Entering another store - I noticed the understanding kind smile on the face of the shop keeper - - Without asking for her assistance - she handed me a 50 dollar note - and asked me to go to the "Drug" store and get a dozen eggs for her - - The drug store - I thot - how queer - the drug store for eggs?? - I asked: where is the Drug store? With a smile she said: "you will find it"---

I walked many blocks one way - - thinking I had gone too far - I turned in another direction - - I walked an equal distance - then I thot: 'I will earn that $50. before I find that store or the eggs' -- Here I met a woman with some sort of a vehicle - like unto a "car" - - I asked the address of the Drug Store - - she very obligingly said: "I will take you to it" - her house - or door - was nearby -- I followed her - - she entered a small compartment - much like a small cubicle - and - she shined her shoes! I waited and waited - my responsibility and mission began to weigh heavy upon me - and I knew I could not depend upon another - not anyone - - - I began to ponder the reason for the $50. So freely entrusted to me - a stranger - and for so little a purchase as a dozen eggs??---

I looked each way for some sign or land-mark - seeing a tower - 4 square - above all the other buildings - I thot - 'that must be the place'- I made my way toward it - - a gust of wind blew the bill from my hand I thot: NO! it cannot BE!! - - - Watching it float high on the breeze - I stood petrified - - the air carried it up and down - finally it came to rest on the opposite side of the street -- I made a dash for it - - the breeze swept it just out of my reach - many times - - finally a little animal - something like a cross between a rabbit and a poodle dog - grabbed the bill - chewed it up - and swallowed it! I grabbed him and opened his mouth - saw his needle-like teeth - thrust my hand down his throat - to my elbow - into his hot stomach and brot forth the bill - opened it up - the teeth holes had penetrated it - making designs - - I thot: "its Holy".-

Then I had to make haste to a temple - which rose high in the air - which I had to enter by climbing many flights of zig-zag stairs - - I had a shopping cart - which I had to leave at the bottom of these stairs -- I knew I must leave my "cart" on public domain (not on private property). After it was carefully parked - I ascended many flights - and looked back - down - to see a man trying to take my cart -- I shouted: "No! No! that is mine!" - he disappeared - - - On gaining the top of the stairs - I entered the temple - thinking: "I shall be late for the sermon". A woman met me in a hallway - - I said: "I am dusty I should like to wash my hands"- she pointed to the pantry or kitchen - where the food for a beautiful banquet had been prepared - - - I wondered why she had admitted me to the "Kitchen" where only the workers should be admitted - - They seemed to be waiting - - - I inquired if I was late for the meeting - - and found that they were expecting me - and the banquet was in my honor - - -

Revealed to Sister Thedra

The Diadem

Sori Sori -- Be ye as one prepared to enter into the place wherein I am. I am as one prepared to receive thee - for this have I bid thee - "Come unto Me" - for this have I given unto thee that which I have deemed wise - that ye might be prepared -- So be it I now say - Come - for I am with thee that ye find thy way into mine place of abode - wherein ye shall stand with me upon mine Holy Mount - and ye shall see wherein ye have been - and that which hast been accomplished ---

Ye shall rejoice that it is finished - done - and ye shall be glad for that which is finished - that which hast been accomplished ---

Ye shall marvel at the wisdom and perfection of the plan which is worked out so perfectly ---

Wherein is it said - that the plan is perfect in all its details - and it is so - for the Father hast so willed it - so - let it be- - for this have I come ---

While it is given unto me to see the plan in its fullness - thou seest in part - as thru the mist - yet it is well - I say - IT IS WELL! - and it is given unto me to know every detail - every step of the way -- And I say unto thee - there is great things in store for the Initiate - for them which follow where I lead ---

I go before thee to prepare the way - and I point out the pitfalls -- I place mine hand upon thee and say - Come follow ye me -- I make sure of the way - and ye have placed thine hand in mine - and obeyed mine every command - now I say unto thee: Thou shall find thine reward - thine reception shall be great - and thy heart shall be made to rejoice - for long hast thou labored in mine vineyard ---

I say: LONG hast thou <u>labored</u> in MINE VINEYARD - and it is now come when ye shall find thine way unto the place of thine going out - and ye shall hear the glad anthem: Welcome! Welcome home thou good and faithful servant ---

I say unto thee: Hail! Hail! Hail unto the Victor - Welcome! Be ye as one blest - for I have blest thee -- So be it I place mine hand upon thy head in Holy Benediction and proclaim thee Prophetess of the ★ and the Shield - and the banner which is mine shall be thine - and ye shall wear the Diadem of the Order of Melchizedek - and ye shall be as one ordained of God the Father - for Greater Service - service beyond thine own mortal ken - which ye remember not - - yet - I say unto thee: Ye shall be caused to remember - and ye shall be glad - for ye shall know, and <u>know</u> that ye know -- So be it The Father's Will.

Will

I say unto thee mine beloved - ye shall return the Victor! So be it and Selah ---

Praise ye the name of Solen Aum Solen - for He is SUPREME - over all - in all - and THE ALL - glorious beyond compare ---

Let thy heart rejoice - be glad that it is come when I might speak unto thee thusly - yet - thou hast not comprehended the fullness of mine words ---

While it is not yet revealed unto thee - the fullness of the plan - I say - ye shall be as one prepared - for at this hour - thou couldst not bear it -- Yet a little while - a little while and I shall take thee, and ye shall be glad ---

While it is yet awhile - I say - there is yet a part which is not finished which shall be finished - - yet it is a lesser part - - and with mine hand in thine - it shall be done with grace and dignity - for it is ordained of

The Father - Which hast initiated THE PLAN -- All is well! All is well! All is well with thee - fear not - praise ye the name of Solen Aum Solen for He is the Father - The All Highest - The Supreme - the Only King of Kings is He -- So be it and Selah ---

Noble are His Sons - Victors are they - Majestic and victorious - for they have fought the fight of the Victor - - for that shall they wear the Crown of the Victor -- I say - they walk the Royal Road - and they know the way unto the Father's House -- These keep open the way - they guard the way - and for that matter they stand ready to serve - and to be the light unto thy feet - that ye stumble not -- Unto them I bow as their servant - for I am the Servant Sent of Mine Father that they be prepared for their part - which they have accepted and proven most worthy -- I say unto them - they shall be glad to receive thee, for one cometh this way which hast fought a good - valiant fight - which hast been found worthy of admittance -- Thy passport is in order - I say - pass within and receive from me thy new part - and there shall be great rejoicing - for long have we waited thy return -- For this are we rejoicing - for this are we glad - let the glad songs ring out - - Hail! Hail! Hail! a Son returns unscathed - unharmed - - Blest is the one which returns unto his place of going out - for he shall wear the Royal Raiment -- Spotless shall be his robes - spotless - I say! Spotless! For he shall return purified - and justified -- Wherein is it said: "He shall be purified and justified"?

Now ye shall come to know what is meant by: "Justified and purified" - for ye shall sit upon mine right hand - and ye shall hold within thine hand the Orb and the Scepter - and ye shall have dominion over the elements - and ye shall go freely into all the secret places - and there have dominion of the elements - and the things ye find therein --

Ye shall be in command of all situations - and no place can there be that shall be closed unto thee - for ye shall be master of all thou shall find to command - - and there shall be no limitation - for ye shall know no limitation -- Now I have spoken wisely and with prudence - knowing that which I say - and I am responsible for mine words ---

I have brot thee out of thy sleep - that I might give unto thee this blessing - this assurance - and thou hast obediently responded unto mine call - mine touch -- Now I say - ye shall add this unto the other records - that they might know that which hast been done - and said - and they shall know in part - yet in part only -- While they bear witness of the written record - they know not the blessing I bring unto thee - for it is thine by Divine Rite -- So be it that a goodly Host attend thee this day -- So be it and Selah ---

Hold ye fast - faint not - let not thy foot slip - I am with thee -- So be it and Selah --

Recorded by Sister Thedra

The Far Fields

Sori Sori -- For this day let it be said - that one shall come unto thee with the authority of the Mighty Council - and he shall give unto thee a part which shall be for the good of all -- He shall bear witness of me of Solen Aum Solen - of thee - and he shall bless them which have prepared themself for to receive of him - for this does he come - so let it be -- I am come that he might be prepared to speak even as I -- So let it be - as the Father has so willed it ---

I come even as mine beloved Sananda - for he hast given unto me that I might come even as he -- So be it that I speak in his name - for the good of all ---

Now let this be recorded in his name - for it shall be as he hast directed ---

When I come unto thee it shall be for the enlightenment of all - and they shall find that first they shall believe - then accept - and then they shall be given as they are prepared -- They shall be <u>shown</u> - they shall know that which they are shown - for this is the day of revelation -- Things shall be revealed unto thee which cannot be written - neither can they be put into words - for they are of the Spirit ---

These things shall pertain unto the SPIRIT - and they shall be of the "Greater Part"- and no words - no pen can convey the fullness of the Spirit ---

While it is most difficult to give the full meaning of earthly things in words - it is more difficult to speak of Spirit - - more difficult to convey in any tongue the great lessons of Spirit -- Therefore it is necessary to lead thee afield - and show thee that which is - and then ye see and know - without any doubt - with no misunderstanding -- These which come unto thee are prepared to lead thee forth with surety of foot - certain of their course - <u>Oneness</u> of purpose - and with the Love of all -- At no time shall they betray themself - or their trust -- They are most efficient - and with great wisdom shall they be given their part - and they shall do their part well - efficiently - for this have they been chosen ---

Let us proceed with our part - and we shall come into a place wherein ye have not been - and ye shall have within your hand the Orb and the Scepter - and ye shall be as one in authority - for ye shall either go farther - or turn back -- Ye shall serve in any capacity which ye choose - for ye shall be as one prepared to choose wisely - and wisely ye shall choose ---

So be it I shall take thee afield - and show unto thee things which ye have not seen - and ye shall give unto them as they are prepared -- I say - ye shall give unto "them" as they are prepared to receive - - so give unto "them" with wisdom and prudence - and they in turn shall know the true from the false ---

When it is come that ye lead them afield - and they have seen and when they know - then they can speak with authority - even as thou canst ---

Now ye shall be as one blest to enter into the place wherein I shall lead thee - and ye shall find therein many new wondrous things which thou hast not imaged - many things new - and wondrous to behold!

Just a while and we shall enter into the field wherein ye shall walk with sure foot - and with eyes that see - and ye shall know that which ye see -- So be it that ye shall know for a surety that which hast been said unto thee ---

Ye shall stand upon The High Holy Mount as one alert - as one prepared for thy "New Part" and ye shall do that which shall be given unto thee with dignity - and with the power and authority invested within thee of Solen Aum Solen ---

For ye shall stand before the Throne of The Most High Living God and receive from Him thy enua - and ye shall go forth even as one with Him ---

Now ye shall go into the "Secret Place" and give unto them as ye have received -- So be it and Selah ---

Hold not thy love and blessing from them - yet - it is said - give with prudence and wisdom - for they shall not be fortuned that which they have NOT prepared themself to receive -- They shall first prepare then they shall be as one on firm ground - a sure foundation ---

Thou hast built thy house on a "Rock" - The "Rock" which shall not be found unfit - - neither shall it be rejected by the "Great Architect"- or Builder ---

I say: The Sure Foundation is that which shall stand forevermore - it shall stand as the Rock of Ages! - which shall not be destroyed by tides - winds - - whereupon thou shall cling in the time of trouble -- So let it be that they shall learn the frailty of their <u>own</u> <u>will</u> - and the Surety of God's Love - and then they shall have Him as their Captain - and their ship shall be brot safely to harbor - and no storm shall beset them for He is sufficient unto all their needs - ALL their NEEDS! - for He knows each by their light ---

Wherein hast it been said that not a sparrow falls unnoticed! Wherein can one hide from Him - their Father?

Be ye as one which can see - hear - know -- I say - let us go - let us know - let us be as one which knows - - and be that which He hast willed ---

Praise ye the name of Solen Aum Solen - for He hast brot us hither. Wait for no man - wait for nought - WAIT NOT!

Come - and be ye blest --

I Am

Recorded by Sister Thedra

Return of the Prodigal Son

Sori Sori -- Oh Mighty Father - there is one which hast her hand in mine which stands at the portal of the Inner Temple - awaiting admittance - I ask that she be admitted on her cognizance - that she be allowed to enter in and partake of Thy Estate - - for she hast been long away - she hast traveled far afield - footsore and weary - she now returns - the Victor ---

She asks that she be admitted in Thy name -- Oh - Father - I have brot her thus far on her own merits - for she hast been obedient in mine sight - and she hast asked not that I carry her burdens on mine back ---

She hast not put her cares upon another - neither has she shifted the blame for her failures or suffering ---

She hast followed where I have led her - Father - and I now bring her unto thee - that Ye might place upon her Thine Benediction - and give unto her Thine Gift - which Thou hast willed unto her -- Let it be given unto her as she is prepared to receive ---

Bless her Father - with Thine Wisdom and Mercy - as Thou hast blest me -- So be it I have added mine unto Thine in Thine name -- So be it and Selah --

I Am Thy Son

Behold ye mine beloved! the Power - the Glory - the Majesty of our Father God - from which all Love flows - all blessings - all wisdom - purity and perfection - - For He is perfection - He is Love - He is Wisdom! So be it I know whereof I speak - therefore mine words shall bear fruit - and I am within mine rightful place -- So be it that ye shall abide with me - and ye shall be glad for thine preparation -- So be it and Selah --

Recorded by Sister Thedra

The Green Nut & The Touch

Sori Sori -- Mine hand is upon thine - and I place mine hand upon thine that it might be as mine hand - that it do that which I would do - that which I will that it do -- So be it that I now give unto thee a part most precious unto the initiate - for he shall know that which I say - and he shall remember his time with me --So be it and Selah ---

I say - there shall be ones which have not the mind to comprehend and they shall not be reminded of mine words - for they are as the "Green Nut"- they have not come to the fullness of their time - they are not as yet ripe/ ready for the touch which I shall place upon them ---

When they are touched they shall come forth as one prepared - as one which shall be glad for mine touch ---

They shall respond unto mine touch - and be as one ready - for it is given unto me to know the green from the ripe - - I pluck not the green that it be left upon the ground to rot -- I say unto thee - I pluck not the green nut - and cast it upon the ground to rot ---

I wait - I wait - and wait - - when it is ripe it responds unto mine touch - then it comes forth in response to mine touch - then it is of value unto me ---

I give unto thee this little parable - that ye might know that which is said within the Temple - that which is true unto the law - for no words can convey that which is of Spirit - which is far beyond the power - the beauty of Earth language -- It is said that truth is conveyed by symbols it is true that thy language is inadequate - and the symbol is of greater value -- While I use the parable to give unto the lessons of the Spirit - I say - they are too symbols - - wherein are they lacking in truth? They are truth indeed - and have I not used them wisely? I say ye understand that which I say - and it is well -- So be it and Selah ---

Recorded by Sister Thedra

The Joy of Attaining

Sori Sori -- This is the day for which thou hast waited -- I say unto thee this is the day for which thou hast waited - - it is now come - and ye shall be as one on whose shoulders rest great responsibility -- Now ye shall say unto them - the time is now at hand - when they shall turn from their willful ways and seek the Light -- They shall be as ones prepared to enter into the Holy of Holies - and they shall be as ones blest that they enter in -- None shall enter the place wherein I Am unprepared - they see not the top of the Mountain - they know not the joy of attaining the summit -- For this do I say: "Prepare thyself" that ye might know as I know! ---

Behold ye the Summit! See ye the Light! Hear ye the loud cry: Hail! Hail! ye Sons of God - - Hail! Hail! Unto the Victor - a Son is risen! - Be ye as one risen - as one lifted up - - for this do I say: "Be ye as one prepared" - behold ye the way of the Lord - for He is become one with thee - He is the Way Shower - and ye shall follow after Him - and He shall lead thee - and ye shall not fall - not fail -- So be it and Selah -- Halt not before the onslaught - for the multitude would trample before thine eyes - the banner which I have set up ---

I come - bringing the Light which they see not -- I come crying: "Behold the Light! See it and be ye one with it - walk ye in it - and be as one which hast received as I have"---

Know ye that the law is just and swift -- Bless thyself to receive of the Father as I have received -- Bless thyself to receive of Him thy Crown of Victory - for by His own hand shall He crown thee Victor - - Lord of all shall ye wear the Crown of Victory ---

Be ye as one blest this day -

I am come that ye be blest -

So let it be --

Recorded by Sister Thedra

Rescue Work

Sori Sori -- There be few that are admitted into the place wherein ye shall go - for few there be - that are prepared to enter in -- I say - few there be which enter in where I take thee - - for this hast thou been prepared -- So be it that the sleepers shall be awakened - and they shall come forth as ones "ripe"- and they shall be blest as thou hast been blest of me -- Now I say: Come - Come with me - and I shall lead thee gently and ye shall not fail - neither shall ye find therein any resting place -- So be it that I shall lead thee gently and <u>firmly</u> -- Ye shall be the one chosen of me for the work at hand - and ye shall know that which ye are to do -- So be it and Selah --

Thedra:- - Now I <u>know</u> my work is rescue work -- My work this night was to go to my grandpa David - and grandma Mary -- She passed from the earth body - after a long time of invalidism -- so did he (years of arthritis and much drugs) -- He was out of his chair when I found him - attended by a "beautiful soul" - a colored man - who had left a good place to come to <u>grandpa</u> -- Grandma was but "skin and bones"- mind alert enuf - - she knew me - and I kissed her and asked for grandpa and she said he was out for a walk - - would return soon - - but she was hungry all the time - -

I never wept so much as I did - it was tears of the heart - - I sat waiting - - Soon the orderly returned with grandpa David - and I was glad he was able to walk - - I was so glad for the attendant - - - - On awakening in my <u>flesh</u> body - I realized this attendant to be a colored servant - who had also loved the family - and had served us for 3 generations - with his family -- How radiant and knowing he is! - he too had gone to get grandpa out of his chair - on his feet -- He (grandpa) wore a dark shimmering blue robe - much like a man's dressing gown here - only of some silk-like material - satin? a very translucent material.

Such is mine word unto thee - pay ye heed - and know ye this: That I am come that ye might KNOW - and it is given unto thee to be as one on which I place mine mantle - and ye shall wear it with dignity and with great responsibility -- So be it and Selah --

Recorded by Sister Thedra

The Way unto the Father's House

Sori Sori -- For this hour let it be recorded for all to read which may - that there is but God The Father - Over all is He - above all is He - and ALL is He - and from HIM -- All life eternal! Cometh from Him - by Him - of Him - and in Him ALL have their Being! "Their Being" I say!

For this is His Being - Which hast sent forth that which exists forever as His own manifestation - His own Person in many forms of manifestation - - Forms of manifestation are many - and none without Life --

That "Life" is His --

Sacred it is to His Body - unto His Economy - therefore I say unto thee: Strange tho it might seem unto thee now - that even unto the lowest form of mineral life - is endowed with intelligence which is of "Him"- - For NO thing is without thot - for thot brings its own form - hast form - and is from the Source ---

Yet I tell thee that there are ones which take the forms sent forth perfect - and abort them -- Think ye that the Father creates the horrors which beset the children of men?

I say unto thee mine own beloved - Nay! Nay! never hast He created such horrors - for He is the PERFECT -- Hast He ever turned His thot from Perfection - - The Perfection of a Great and Grand Plan - which His little children comprehendeth not - NOT - I say! for they are as the new born child - - into the world they come - helpless - and in so short a time they come out - as ones born again into yet greener fields - with the greater vistas - greater visions - greater knowledge - and a greater capacity for understanding - - I say: "A greater capacity for understanding!" And as they grow into maturity - their understanding of HIM increases in proportion unto their preparation -- So be it the law of Being - so let it be as He hast willed it ---

When it is come that ye stand with me upon mine "High Holy Mount" ye shall see and know as I know - and ye shall have the Greater Vision -- Then ye shall see as I see - and ye shall do that which I do - for then ye shall Know that which I Know - for ye shall be as I AM - and ye shall walk as I walk - knowing thou art of The Father - in Him secure - and forever staid in Him ---

Let it be understood that He is All - THE ALL -- Without Him nothing exists - no thing! for He encompasseth all which IS - both manifest and unmanifest - therefore He is over all - above all - and within all - and He is the Giver and the Taker -- He gives - and He takes away ---

Now ye shall ponder well mine words -- Think ye not that I speak idly - neither do I give unto thee foolish sayings - for I am not a "fool".

I speak from the higher vantage point - therefore I say unto thee mine beloved: bear in mind that I see and know whereof I speak ---

Art thou not within mine keeping - art thou not of mine fold - art thou not in mine care - have I not said - I shall not forsake thee - that I shall lead thee thru the dark valleys and thru the desert lands - wherein they wait - athirst and hungry?---

Now it is come when I shall show unto thee great things - and ye shall rejoice that thou hast been so privileged to see - and to know --

Yet thou hast dared the abyss - dared the shadows dark and foreboding -- Now ye shall gain the Greater Vision - for I say unto thee thou hast not turned aside - neither hast thou said me - nay! - - Thou hast firmly placed thine own hand in mine - as a little child - and followed where I have lead thee -- Now - I say - come forth and I shall show unto thee great wonders - wonders beyond thine own imagining for thine eyes hast not beholden such vistas!

Neither hast thine eyes beheld such glory as I shall unveil unto thee.

Thy suffering hast been great - thy waiting long - yet thou hast endured for <u>mine</u> sake -- Thou hast heard mine voice - and responded unto it - now I say unto thee: Ye shall find thine reward to be great - for all thy suffering - and thy waiting shall be as nothing - for thine tears shall be as jewels which shall reflect the Love of the Father - Which hast Sent Me -- So be it and Selah ---

I say - it is now come when thy hand shall be set to greater tasks - greater things shall ye do - for this shall be the "Greater Part"- and ye shall <u>not</u> <u>fail</u> - neither shall ye want - for I shall direct thee - and lead thee - and I KNOW the Way ---

So be it I have walked the way in which I bid thee - I am the "Wayshower" and I have bidden thee: "Come - follow Me." And thou hast forsaken all to follow after me - and thou hast not flinched - neither hast thou cried out in thy hours of testing - - Yea - testing there hast been - testing? Yea - testing!

Wherein wast it said: "Ye shall be tested as in the furnace?" I say - thou hast been tested! And thou hast not flinched - neither hast thou cried out: "let me go!"

I say unto thee mine beloved: Thou hast been tested - thine strength hast been tested - thine will hast been tested - and thine motives - thine every act - thine every thot! - - Yet I say - thou hast dared the canyons the valleys of despair - the steeps - the depths - - the daring hast been thine strength - for thine daring is thine strength!

The gifts which have been bestowed upon thee art three fold - they are as - the gift of the Spirit - the gift of understanding - the gift of communication ---

Now ye shall have another added unto the three - for these hast served thee well - thou hast used them well - and thou shall find the fourth added as one unto the other hast been added - and they together shall be as one - used for the glory of God the Father -- And none shall pilfer - neither shall they take from thee one - nor the other - for they shall be thine by the Sacred Decree - the mandate of the Mighty Council that which is over All -- That which is of the Mighty Council cannot be set aside by man - for it is the mandate of God-The-Father - and no man hast the power or the authority to set aside His Mandate ---

Be ye as one prepared to enter into the Inner Temple - and I bid thee enter -- For this have I led the out - for this have I given unto thee of mineself that the Word be made manifest upon the Earth - that His Glory be seen - be made manifest -- So be it and Selah ---

As I have spoken - so hast it been recorded -- So let it stand for all time - for it shall not be erased from the "Book of Life" ---

Blest shall they be which do read the pages upon which this is written -- So be it and Selah --

Recorded by Sister Thedra

The Admonition

Sori Sori -- By mine own hand shall I lead thee into the place wherein I am - and ye shall stand upon mine High Holy Mount as one with me and ye shall walk with me and counsel with me - and ye shall do that which shall be given unto thee to do ---

While it is now come that ye have been given a part which is new unto thee - ye shall be as one responsible for that part - for it is thine -- The gift of free will hast been given of the Father - and now thou hast been given the gift of service wherein I am - and ye have accepted it in His name -- So be it ye shall do HIS WILL - and ye shall be accountable for that which ye do with this "Gift"-- Ye shall not be as a traitor - ye shall walk with assurance - ye shall be as one on whose head I have placed mine hand - and unto which I have spoken with the authority which is mine - the words of Holy Benediction -- And ye shall know that which I say unto thee is THE WORD OF TRUTH pure and

UNCONTAMINATED - for I say unto thee: nothing shall adulterate the line of communication between us - for I have prepared thee well - I have kept this line of communication open - and I say unto thee: The way of the Lord is made clear before thee ---

I have gone before thee and I have cleared the way - yet it is said - be ye as one mindful of thy part - and be ye watchful - for there are none which enter herein unprepared -- For this I would admonish thee: Prepare thyself for to enter into the Holy of Holies wherein I abide ---

I have said unto thee: Thine passport is in order - yet - "There are many slips between the cup and the lips" -- So - be ye as one obedient unto mine commandments - and harken unto mine touch - and I shall lead thee every step of the way ---

Blest are they which enter in -- Blest are they - for they shall see God - they shall have their inheritance in full -- Praise ye the NAME of Solen Aum Solen - for He is the Source of thy Being --

Recorded by Sister Thedra

Wait for the Harvest

Sori Sori -- This day it is said that there shall be a great awakening - and it is so - so let it be - - for this have I made known mine presence in the world of man---

This is the day long foretold - yet there are the sleepers which sleep sleep the sleep of the dead -- I say - these are as the living dead - they know not that I am come - that I am present ---

They wait for the "Judgement Day"- - I say - they wait - for the judgement day ---

They are as the "Green nut"- not as yet prepared for harvest -- While they wait - I too wait - I await them to ripen -- I pluck not the green nut from its branch aforetime - for they would be of no use unto me - they would be cast aside as unfit for mine service - or use - - So be it I wait.

Bear ye in mind that I know the ripe from the green - and I pluck not the green nut from the branch - for it would be poor judgment - and of no profit -- Such is mine word - and it is so - so let it be - for this hast it been given unto thee - - Wait for the harvest - and it shall profit thee ---

Place thine hand in mine and I shall lead thee - and direct thee - and ye shall not go astray - for mine work shall be thine - thine time shall be mine - and ye shall have the way of the Lord before thee - and ye shall know that which lies ahead -- So be it I have gone before thee that ye fall not -- So be it I am the Light - and the Way -- Amen and Selah

Recorded by Sister Thedra

Sori Sori -- Be ye as one responsible for that which shall be given unto thee to do - for ye shall go forth as one prepared - - and ye shall be as one anointed - and as one prepared -- So be it and Selah ---

Now ye shall be as one which hast received mine hand - and as one which hast heeded mine word - and for this have I placed about thee mine mantle - and ye shall wear it with dignity - and ye shall not fail.

I say unto thee - wear it - and be ye as one alert - and fear not - for I am with thee -- So be it and Selah--

The Green Nut & The Builder

Sori Sori -- For this hour let it be given unto thee to record these words which shall be given unto them which seek the Light - which are of a mind to follow after me ---

This is mine word unto them: The way which I have gone is open unto them - it is the sure and strait way - the safe way -- And it is given unto me to be the Guardian of the Way - the "Keeper of the Gate" -- Therefore - I say that none enter unprepared - - so be it that I am come that all might be prepared ---

Yet - there are ones which seek in the dark halls of experiences for that which the senses crave - that which they so willingly ask to receive which they accept without question - - yet they question ME - and mine authority!

They ask proof of me?!

And wherefore have I disavowed mine own power - the authority bestowed upon me by mine Father which hast Sent Me - that they might suffer no more?

Now - mine beloved - I say unto thee: These are as the green nut - they shall ripen - and as they come - they shall ripen and come forth as ones prepared to serve me - as ones of value in mine work - - then - they shall be fit for use ---

They shall be filled with flavor and be of value unto me -- Think not that I speak frivolity - for I know that which I say ---

I speak clearly - and with meaning - - I am not given unto frivolity.

For that matter - I have given unto thee the parable of "The Builder" which I AM ---

I have said that the builder casts aside the rotten timber - he rejects the unfit - and uses only that which is prepared - that which is <u>good</u> and substantial ---

He sees the good - which he can use - and likewise he sees that which is unfit for the construction of the "Temple" ---

Now it is fortuned unto me to be the Builder of the Temple - and it behooves me to say unto thee - come ye forth as one prepared - for I have need of thee - - I have need of thee -- I say - Come - be ye as one prepared - and when thou hast prepared thineself - I shall do mine part I shall take thine hand and lead thee into the place wherein there are things which thou hast not seen - which shall serve thee in greater measure - and wherein ye shall be as one prepared for the greater part these things I shall do - and greater!

These things shall I reveal unto thee in the measure of thine own strength and preparation -- It is for this that I have said - lay aside all thine preconceived ideas and opinion - - for this have I said - I shall touch thee and ye shall be made to see - and ye shall <u>know</u> that which ye see ---

So be it that I come - and I bless them which are prepared to receive me - and mine own -- The WORD have I given that they prepare themself - and I stand as one prepared to do mine part ---

No man can paint the glory of the place which I have prepared for them which come unto Me -- When ye have entered into the Holy of Holies ye shall see as I see - ye shall be blest as I am blest -- So be it that I shall be as one prepared to receive thee - and in like manner - shall ye receive them which shall follow thee -- So let it be - and so shall it be - and for this I am glad --

Recorded by Sister Thedra

The Gift & Obligation

Sori Sori -- By mine own hand shall I lead thee - - by mine own hand shall I lead thee out of bondage - - by mine own hand shall I direct thee So be it and Selah ---

Ye shall now fashion for thyself greater - and even greater mansions for I shall bring unto thee one which hast within his hand the power and the authority to give unto thee a new gift - a gift which shall serve the people which shall profit them ---

Yea - it shall be for the good of all - and it shall be as none other gift which I have given - for it shall be different from mine gifts ---

I say - One shall I bring unto thee which shall give unto thee his gift which shall be for the good of all mankind -- So be it and Selah ---

Ye shall be as one prepared to receive of him - his gift - - and it shall be that he hast come in the name of the Father Which hast Sent Me - and by the consent of the Mighty Council does he come ---

Now ye shall receive him even as thou hast received Me --

Sori Sori -- I come in the name of mine beloved Brother - even as he comes in the name of our Father Which hast given unto us being ---

Ye shall be as one blest of us - even as we are blest by Him Which hast sent us -- In His name do we come ---

Behold ye the hand of God - see it <u>move</u> - and rejoice that this day is come - when we might commune - even as the Council which now sits for the good of All -- Let our communication be profitable unto all for this is the beginning of a new part of the plan - which shall be unfolded unto thee part by part - portion by portion ---

Ye shall be given the strength - the power - and time - to do that which is demanded of thee - and ye shall not want -- So be it that I come that ye receive of me a gift which shall be added unto thine others - which shall be used to glorify our Father Which is over all - Which is THE ALL - O -- So be it that I place upon thine head mine hand - and I pronounce the Word which shall be unto thee the "Key" - thy passport the authority to use - to have - to hold - and ye shall use it wisely - and justly at all times -- Ye shall have the power - and the authority to use it - and ye shall be as one responsible for the misuse of it -- This responsibility shall weigh heavily upon thy shoulders - - yet - I say unto thee: Thou hast dealt justly with them which have come unto thee - and thou hast proven trust worth - and ye shall be as one proven/ tried as by fire! - and ye shall be as one prepared by fire - - ye shall stand upon the Rock Which shall be thy sure footing ---

Let it be said that I am come by the command of the Mighty Council for it is thru the Council that I come unto thee -- Ye shall bear witness of me - and ye shall come to know me - even as ye know the Beloved Sananda Which is my constant companion ---

I say - HE is mine constant companion - - Ye shall bear witness unto mine words - for they shall be unto thee great power and strength.

Now ye shall go forth as a soldier unto battle - in full armor - for ye shall go in confidence - and ye shall be as one in shining armor -- Ye shall wear thine credentials as a diadem upon thy brow ---

Ye shall grovel unto no man - for ye shall be as one apart - and separate from them - - ye shall stand tall! And I say unto thee - ye shall not bow unto any man - neither shall ye solicit favor from any man ---

Ye shall be steadfast - and ye shall be as one on whose shoulders is placed the Cloak of Authority - - ye shall go forth as one Knowing - and ye shall be as one in authority ---

Ye shall not stumble - neither shall ye fall - - ye shall bless others as thou hast been blest ---

Ye shall sit in high places and counsel with them - and ye shall be unafraid ---

Now ye shall be mindful of these mine words - and that which I endow unto thee -- So be it I place upon thine head mine hand in Holy Benediction - and I pronounce thee A - - - - in thine own right -- And it shall be that I shall shield thee with mine Cloak - Mine Armor for a time - and within that time ye shall learn to walk with sure feet - and ye shall grow in strength and knowledge---

Now ye shall be as one blest to see that which ye have not seen - and hear that which ye have not heard - and for this shall thy knowledge be expanded beyond that which thou hast had -- Ye shall now know that which thou hast known in part only - in proportion to thine gifts -- Now another is added unto that which hast been given unto thee - - So be it profitable unto thee -- use it wisely - and for the good of all mankind ---

So be it that I have spoken of thy gift - yet I have not openly spoken of that which ye shall do - - yet ye shall know that which ye shall do with such a gift - which carries with it great responsibility!

GREAT RESPONSIBILITY I SAY!!

Bear in mind that I too - have a responsibility unto thee - for the gift which I have passed on unto thee - for it is the JEWEL WITHOUT PRICE ---

Upon thine heart ye shall wear it - and ye shall treasure it as thine own life - - bear in mind - it is thy Great Treasure -- Upon thy head ye shall have the Star - and ye shall be known by that Star in the day to come - for it shall shine forth as the Morning Star -- And none shall be the lesser - neither the greater - for seeing - or seeing not -- yet I say - ye shall be known by that Star which shall be thine - and it shall be as none other ---

While I say it shall be as none other - I too say - that there shall be others - yet no two shall be alike -- Ye shall likewise know them which wear the Star upon their forehead - for ye shall see them as we see them and by the Star shall ye know each other ---

While I say ye shall know each other by the Star emblazoned upon the forehead - I too say: Ye shall sit in counsel - and ye shall know that which is to be done - that which shall go forth - - and it shall be revealed unto man - that which is done thru and by the Council ---

While it is not yet time to reveal ALL the plan - it shall be revealed in part - - and they shall come to know there IS a PLAN ---

So be it I withdraw - and I shall leave thee with mine own blessing ever mindful of mine trust and obligation unto thee --

Recorded by Sister Thedra

The Battle

Sori Sori -- Hear ye me - and be ye as one prepared to go forth as a warrior unto the battle - for it shall be a battle! - and one not easily won.

There are forces beyond thy comprehension - which are at work - which would tear down that which we of the Mighty Council build up And it is for this that I say: "Go ye forth as one prepared to do battle!"

Behold ye the HAND of God - see it move - and know that it sustains thee - it shall uphold thee ---

By His Hand shall ye be upheld - for there is none that shall say Him - "Nay!" for He is the Greatest/ Over All/ and He shall reign supreme! forever and forever -- So be it and Selah --

Sori Sori -- This day ye shall see the Hand of God move - and ye shall be glad - for I say unto thee - that it moveth in strange ways - ways which thou hast not considered - ways which thou hast not known -- Ye shall behold the work of the Lord - for thine eyes shall be made to see as they have not seen -- Ye shall be glad for thy seeing - for thou shall see the fruits of thy work - and ye shall know that it hast been profitable -- Ye shall stand with me and survey the work of thy hand - the labor of thy hand shall be as the rosary - and ye shall count each as a blessing - one after another ye shall add unto the other - yet ye shall not be finished ---

Ye shall see that which hast been accomplished and ye shall say: "Blest is the name of Him which hast sent me - for the plan is revealed unto me"---

Therefore I say unto thee - hold ye steadfast and follow ye me - and I shall direct thee in all thy ways - - ye shall add the note which is before thee - and ye shall find it well indeed to enter it into the record --

Recorded by Sister Thedra

For the Record

Sori Sori -- Be ye as one responsible for that which I give unto thee to do - and ye shall be as one on whose shoulders rests great responsibility for I shall give unto thee a greater part - - so be it ye shall not fail - neither shall ye want -- I am with thee and I am responsible for mine part - let it be -- Let it be that this part shall profit thee - and ye shall come unto this altar again this day for another part for them which await it --

* * *

Sori Sori -- Let it go down in these records - that all might see and know that which hast been said unto thee - for it shall prove great power unto them ---

Now I say - as hast been said before - that it is with the consent of the Mighty Council that I come unto thee - and ye shall come to know me even as ye know my Beloved Sananda ---

While it is yet not time for all things to be revealed unto thee - I say in due season ye shall know as I know - - ye shall be blest as I have been blest -- So be it and Selah - - for I have gone the selfsame road - I have given of myself that others be prepared - even as I was ---

Now let it be recorded - that it is for this that I am permitted to come unto thee - that ye be prepared to enter into the Inner Temple -- So be it and Selah -- I entreat thee to hold fast - fear not - waver not - and ye shall pass within the portal unscathed - - let not thine foot slip - let thine heart feel no sorrow -- Give unto me thine hand and I shall lead thee - for I am one of them which are responsible for thy safety - thru the dark chambers thru which ye shall pass -- Let it be for thy own safety that I offer mine assistance - and let it profit thee to accept mine assistance - So shall we go forward as one - one in peace - in harmony - and one in purpose - So let it be as the Father hast willed it --

Recorded by Sister Thedra

The Blessing

Sori Sori -- Fortune thyself the greater part - and for this have we - thine guardians said unto thee: "Prepare thyself" - - for this have we offered our assistance -- Let it profit thee - for it is given unto us to know that which is before thee -- Say unto them as we say unto thee: Arise and come forth from thy valley of despair - and walk ye upright - and be ye as one which can see the way in which ye should go ---

Let them which have ears hear - - let them which have eyes see - - and be ye as one responsible for thy part -- Let them be as ones responsible for their part -- Thine part is to give unto them as I give unto thee - - it is their part to receive as thou hast received -- So be it that they shall follow willingly and joyfully -- So be it the way is plainly marked before them - and they which choose shall find it the safe and sure way -- So be it that I stand by as one prepared to assist -- for this have I been prepared ---

Bless them which come unto thee - bless them which ask of thee - and ye shall be blest in like measure -- So be it and Selah ---

When they come as ones prepared - ye shall give unto them the part which shall profit them -- When they come as ones rebellious - ye shall withhold it - and speak unto them that which shall be suitable unto them that which they can comprehend - and send them away with nothing - for they but give nothing - - they are as ones seeking self-aggrandizement -- and for that matter they are not prepared to enter into the Inner Temple -- So be it that I have said - they are responsible for that which they do with the word - it is so -- Therefore they shall find that it is not to be held lightly! it is sacred indeed - therefore not to be desecrated!

Therefore handle it not lightly! for it shall rebound upon thee -- Sanctify thine work - protect it - and fear not the scorn of the profane - Let them plant their feet upon solid ground - and wait for that which shall be their portion - -

Recorded by Sister Thedra

The Prodigal

Sori Sori -- This word I would give unto thee at this time - - let it be understood that when one comes into the place wherein I am - they shall be as one prepared - and they shall stand as one with me - and they shall be as one blest of me - and by me they shall be blest ---

For this shall be the part which I am given - - to receive them and to bless them as I have been blest -- Wherein is it said that I shall do mine part --

While it is given unto me to have the greater part - it shall be given unto me to give unto thee as I have received -- So be it and Selah ---

Behold ye the hand of God - see it move - and be ye blest to receive lo - I am come that ye receive -- While it is not yet come that ye receive the greater part - I say ye shall be blest to receive -- So be it I shall stand before the Throne of the Father - and give unto thee as HE hast given unto me -- He shall give unto thee as thou art prepared to receive --

Now it is come when He hast placed within mine own hands the power to bestow upon thee thy enua - and it is said that thine inheritance shall be complete/ in full - and ye shall rejoice forevermore - - Ye shall stand as one glorified - as one purified - and justified -- So be it and Selah --

Recorded by Sister Thedra

The Meeting of the Waters

Sori Sori -- Bear in mind that the time is come when the things which hast been hidden shall be revealed unto thee - and there shall be even greater revelation than thou hast dreamed -- So be it that I am come that ye might have Light! Light! I say! For this is mine part - to give unto thee the Greater gifts - the gifts of the SPIRIT which no man can take from thee ---

Now it is come when ye shall see and know that which hast been hidden - that which thou hast not seen -- Yet thou hast followed me - and I have led thee gently - and wisely -- Thou hast given me thine hand and thine heart - and I have favored thee - - for that matter - I have set thee apart - and given unto thee the authority to speak in mine name - and that ye might not fail - I have walked with thee into the places unknown unto thee - and I have safeguarded thee -- Yet - thou hast not turned aside nor cried out -- Now I say unto thee - ye shall do even greater things than these -- Ye shall be as one prepared for greater things/ greater responsibility! and ye shall not be afraid - neither shall ye weary - - neither shall ye want - for I shall be thine hand and thine foot ---

Wait upon me - the Lord thy God - and I shall lead thee - and ye shall do that which I give unto thee to do - and ye shall become strong in thy weak parts -- Ye shall become sufficient unto thyself - for I shall be thy strength and thy stay -- So be it and Selah ---

Fortune thyself the gift of Spirit - and bless thyself - that ye might bless others as I bless thee -- For this have I called thee out from them which have not heard - or - heeded mine voice - - mine call hast gone forth as a loud trumpet - yet they heed not ---

Yet - I call unto each and every one - - few there be which put one foot before the other - or extend their hand that they might give unto me as I have given unto them ---

Play well thy part - and I shall add unto thy gifts threefold --

Ye Shall Do Mine Work

Sori Sori -- Be ye as one prepared to lift them up -- It is said - ye shall do the work I do - - ye shall be as one prepared to go where I go - and it shall be given unto thee to do that which I shall give unto thee to do.

Let this be recorded as the Word of God which shall not pass away and at no time shall it be given unto me to withhold my hand from them which are prepared to receive it -- So be it that I stand ready to give unto them as they are prepared to receive -- So be it and Selah ---

Be ye as one prepared to give unto them as I give unto thee - for this is mine word unto thee this day: Ye shall do mine work - - for this hast it been said: "Great shall be thine service unto them"-- Now it is come when ye shall pass amongst them as I pass - and ye shall see and know that ye are the servant of the Lord Sent - ye shall be blest to

KNOW -- So be it that I have put mine hand upon thy head in Holy Benediction - and I have pronounced thy name - and it shall be recorded in the annals of history that which I have said - for these words shall not perish from the Earth ---

It is well - for it is so decreed that they shall endure -- So be it and Selah ---

Whereupon I set mine seal unto these words - that they may be preserved thruout the generations to follow---

Praise ye the Name of Solen Aum Solen - that He hast given unto thee the mind to comprehend - and to endure -- So be it and Selah --

Recorded by Sister Thedra

THE HOUSE OF THE LORD

= First Part =

Sori Sori -- The hour is come when ye shall begin this new part - and it shall begin with this part -- Let it be the first part - - it shall be called "The House of The Lord" - and it shall be the Word of the Lord God -- While others shall speak within the allotted time - the Word shall go forth with Mine Seal upon it - and none shall be unto Me Censor - for I am Mine own porter - and I bring with Me the Ones which shall speak - even as I - and they shall not be without honor - for they have been as Ones prepared for to come unto thee even as I --

Now ye shall receive them in Mine Honor - and they shall bear witness of Me - and I shall bear witness of them -- So be it and Selah - -

These are Mine Brethren - Mine Family - Mine hands - Mine feet - for they do that which is given unto them to do -- They function as One with Me - even as Mine hand and foot -- They go where Sent - and do that which is necessary -- So be it they are One with Me - and it is for that that We come as One - - in concert We come --

This is the Word We bring at this time: Poor in Spirit are they which deny Us - which deny The Host - - the Spirit of the "Host" they speak of - yet they know not which they say --

They are prone to forget the meaning of the "Host" - which wast spoken of - and which spoke unto them so long ago -- And for that matter - many deny the Word of the Host - while others speak of the

Host - and prattle of the power thereof - - they have not experienced the power thereof --

This I would have them consider: The "Host" is no less this day - than on that day long ago - when they spoke in tongues -- This is the day foretold -- This is the day when the "Host" shall visit them - one by one - two by two*- and in great numbers -- Many shall visit them - even as I shall visit them which are prepared to receive Me -- Yet the Host shall be as ones prepared to go before Me - and "they"** shall be prepared to receive Me --

This is the way in which it shall be accomplished: The Host shall go forth as Ones prepared to touch them which now sleepeth - the ones which are not aware of the Plan - the ones which have not known Me - neither of the Host - unto them which know not that I am come -- "They" shall be as ones quickened - and "they" shall come to know - then "they" shall come forth as ones prepared for a part within the Great Plan--

I say: "Within the Great Plan" - for there is a plan - and it shall be revealed unto them which are prepared to receive -- So be it and Selah -- The plan shall be revealed to each and every one which is so prepared -- So be it that I come declaring that it is now come - when the Host goes forth to awaken them which are prepared to awaken -- The Call hast gone forth: "Awaken! Awaken! Awaken!

The sleepers shall awaken! -- and it is said: They have slept overtime - and it is so -- So be it that the "dead" shall be as ones quickened - and "they" too shall arise and come forth in due season -- So be it and Selah --

I would have thee Know that each unto his own season - each unto his own - - and it is said: Ye shall not fret for them which stir not - - ye shall be as one about thine own affairs - and as one prepared to do that which is given unto thee to do -- Be ye as one blest to hear that which I say unto thee - and ye shall give unto them that which I give unto thee for them -- So be it ye shall keep for thyself that which I give unto thee for thyself - lest they rend thee -- So be it and Selah --

Blest be the hand which does the Work of The Father - the Will of The Father -- Blest is the one which does His Will -- So be it and Selah --

*Individuals - few - or many

**"they" in quotes - refers to ones in flesh

The Bond

Sori Sori -- By Mine own hand ye shall be blest -- So be it and Selah --

The fortune which is Mine shall be thine - and ye shall be blest as I have been blest --

This is Mine Word unto thee at this hour: There are ones which come unto thee for the purpose of directing and guiding thee in the way of the Wise - - these are of the Host - which are gathered together as One - with such Power as thou to hast not known - the Power endowed unto them of The Mighty Council - The Council of Councils --

Now ye shall stand as One with them - and ye shall be as One with them - for it is given unto Me to be the Host of the Host - and I see thee as One with them -- Thy part is within the place wherein ye are - and ye shall come and go as one free in Spirit - and ye shall return unto them - and give unto them assistance - even as ye have received -- Ye shall be as the one which Knows wherein thou art stayed - and ye shall not fail -- This is the time of going out and coming in - and ye shall pass within the walls of the Great and Grand Temple wherein there are many to instruct thee - - and <u>then</u> ye shall give instruction unto the ones so prepared to receive --

While the written Word is designed to prepare them for the Greater unwritten Word - Work - - they shall first accept the written Word - and the Servant which brings it forth - for the "Servant" and the Word shall be as One - - and I say: the "Servant" is One with Me - there is no separation - - for this hast I given unto thee passport --

I give not Mine enemy passport into Mine place of abode -- I give not the puny priest which <u>thinks</u> himself wise passport - for he but thinks to pilfer Mine Store - he but spills the vials of perfume - which he hast no knowledge of - - he but despoils that which he would pilfer -- I say: He shall be as one <u>prepared</u> to enter into Mine place of abode -- So be it and Selah --

Beloved:- Ye shall do a Mighty Work while they sleep - for it is with the Spirit that ye work - for the Spirit is that which is of the Greatest concern - the Spirit of man --

This is the part which is given unto thee - the part which is the Greater part -- While the physical part is but the temporary part of man - it is the lesser part -- Know ye well that the Spirit is the everlasting man - the indestructible man -- While man inhabits the temple of flesh - he appears to be flesh - yet he is more - he is the master over flesh -- "The master of the house of clay" - which he thinks himself to be - is the eternal - eternal verity --

The way in which man goes determines his destiny - - and the way in which he goes is his own choice - for it is given unto man to have free will - and he hast but to choose his own way - and not any man hast a right to say him nay - - he is the one to choose his way --

While it is said: "Ye shall be a light unto thy brothers feet" - it is to thy honor - and it behooves thee to choose the Light - and follow it that thy own path be lighted from the Eternal Light which fails not -- So be it that I am come that ye might Know the Way - and it behooves Me to lead thee safely and surely -- So be it that I ask of thee nought save obedience unto the law --

Come ye - follow where I lead thee - and ye shall find many wondrous things in which to rejoice - and Praise The Father Solen Aum Solen --

Justice

Sori Sori -- Justice shall be meted out unto them which follow Me -- There shall be few which shall not follow - - these shall find Justice - for they shall be as the traitors - they shall find they have betrayed themself - and they too shall find Justice rendered according to their preparation -- They shall be as ones prepared for the Greater part - or they shall accept the lesser --

This is the Law -- While there are ones which strive for the lesser part - they weary of the Greater striving - the striving for the Greater part -- they seek things - work for things - while they fail to seek the Light -- They weary of Mine Sayings - put them aside as of no value - no consequence - and they look for signs and wonders - shining ornaments which glitter - - they are as children looking for attractive toys - - let them find --

They shall find that which they seek - this is the law-- While the toys and glitter shall pass - the law shall remain - and the Light which NEVER FAILS shall be the Light -- It shall profit them to seek that which is Eternal --

The Light Eternal shall be the Light - always - without fail - - whereas the material things shall pass and be no more -- So it is said: "Seek ye the Light - fret not over small things - and be ye as ones prepared for Greater things"

I speak unto all which have ears to hear and eyes to see -- So be it it shall profit thee to hear - and be prepared for yet Greater Glory --

The Glory of which I speak is not of man - not of Earth - it is of The Eternal Verities -- So be it and Selah --

Wait no longer - accept that which is proffered unto thee this day - and let it suffice thee that I am come - declaring the Truth - and pointing unto thee the Way - - seek ye - and ye shall find --

= Dedication =

Let thine hand be Mine - thine Voice be Mine - and let it profit thee -- Let thy time be Mine - let thine way be Mine - - for this do I say: "Come

- follow ye Me" -- Hear ye Me - and be ye as one prepared to follow where I lead thee -- Come let us enter into the Holy of Holies and rejoice forever -- So be it - and so may it be --

Life - Light

Sori Sori - Let this be known among all men - that they be as ones prepared for the Greater School of Life -- Life is not but a flicker of a flame within the dark - which is but a spark here - and gone forever to be seen no more --

Life IS - Life is Life - forever does it exist - with many facets - many aspects - - many times does life circle and make its return unto its abiding place --

Many go out again and again - renewing - refreshing - and returning again into the many created mansions wherein there is form - - various are the forms - many forms Life takes upon itself - yet ALL IS LIFE - - Life - One Substance - Light --

Light and Life are synonymous - and it shall ever BE -- Life more abundant shall ye have / Know - for it is not limited to or in form -- Form is for yea -- form is - yet form is not Life - - Life animates the form --

Form is but the manifestation of the Word -- The Word made manifest in the world of man - is but the Spirit of thot - like unto the thot which holds the manifestation for a time -- At the time of its maturity - the form is released - even as the pea from the pod when it is ripened -- The form too has a time - a season - then it too drops - and returns unto its place of beginning - and no more does that form come forth as once it was -- Yet there are others of its kind which shall come forth from the same elements --

Therefore it is said - that all living things shall be as removed from the Earth -- It is said that man shall inherit the Earth - and all things shall be made new - it is So -- Yet wherein is it said that man shall be burdened with the pestilence of the Earth in his inheritance? Wherein is it said that he shall be as he is now known? For he too shall Know his true identity - and he shall not be bound in flesh - for he shall be free - free to go and come as a true Son of God --

So be it that he shall read aright the "Signs of the times" - and he shall fear not! - for he is his own engineer - he prepares the foundation upon which he shall build his house - - his own architect he shall be - his own draftsman - for he hast the plans before him - he hast been given the law - the tools - the choice -- Now he shall select his sight - his method - his material - his time - and unto this shall be added - his labor -- So be it and Selah --

I have spoken - - let them consider that which I have said - - let them not change Mine Word to suit themself - for the meaning is clear unto them which walk in the Way which I point -- So be it it shall profit them to learn of Me -- So be it and Selah --

Hope

Sori Sori -- The place is here - the time is Now - and it is given unto thee to be as one prepared to receive Me and of Me -- This is the hour of our communion - when we shall commune one with the other -- This shall be the time and the place - while it is not yet day - neither is it night - for this is the hour before daybreak while they sleep - it is the hour when there is less confusion within the Earth's atmosphere - and "they" are at rest -- While "they" rest - We shall come unto thee with such as shall profit the ones which sleep --

That which hast been shown unto thee is for thy own good - thine own sake - yet it behooves Me to say unto thee: Be ye as one prepared to give unto them that which is for them - and that which is shown unto thee - keep for thyself - for it is for thee --

There is but wisdom in this - for they would but rend thee - - they would but fear and smear - and hear not that which is said -- Let them learn and earn - and it shall profit them -- Be ye as one profited by thine own learning --

This I would say unto them which are now adrift - now afloat upon the sea of despair - - they shall be rescued - they shall be brot out -- Let thy hand rest in Mine - and I shall be sufficient unto thee - for I shall send a Host unto thy rescue -- Be ye not dismayed - neither be ye disconsolate - for there are many which stand by to give unto thee a hand -- So be it and Selah --

Be ye as one blest to receive the hand of them which reach out unto thee in the hour of thy trials and thy temptations -- Fear not - for it is now the twelfth hour - and it is now come when Great changes shall take place - and ye shall profit thereby -- So be it and Selah --

= Accuracy & Promptness =

Sori Sori -- The Word of God is that which precedes the manifestation - - the manifestation follows the WORD -- So be it that the Word hast gone forth: Awaken! - and it shall be as done --

While man lives within the world of time and space - distance is of great importance unto him - - while We of the Host are not bound by time or distance - We come as on wings of thot - and We are not bound by time --

It is said: Ye shall be prompt - and it behooves thee to be accurate - and prompt - for this is part of thy preparation - and it is for this that I have said: Be ye as one prompt - for it is for the good of all that each one knows his time - place and part --

Yet ye shall not fret for the time yet to come - ye shall make haste this day - to do that which is before thee - and remember - the morrow shall be as nought - - this day is thy concern -- So be it and Selah -- Let it profit thee to be about thy task of preparation - - fret not for trivialities - for they shall pass as nought -- So be it that I am come that the way be made clear before thee - and ye have but to follow where I lead thee -- Be ye as one alert unto that which goes on about thee - for it is the time of awakening - when many shall bear witness of the Coming - and the awakening -- So be it and Selah --

Man's Sojourn in Flesh

This Mine Word is valid - and I proclaim a day of awakening - when man shall put forth his hand and touch Mine - then I shall bring him forth - and he shall no more touch the pricks which hast held him fast - - he shall no more be torn by the thorns of flesh --

The story of man's sojourn in flesh is indeed a sad and bloody one - - yet he shall come to know that which hast bound him -- He shall break his bounds - and walk as a free man - man free from bondage - free from the fetters which hast bound him --

I say unto him: Awaken! - he hast begun to stir - yet he falls again and again - for he is as yet not awake - fully awake - wherein he knows himself for that which he is -- He fears that he is <u>not</u> the one which he thinks himself to be - and he knows not which TO THINK! for he is confused! This is the day of confusion for man - - yet let it be said: There is no confusion within the place wherein I am - for We Know that which We are about - that which is given unto us to do - and that which We shall do -- By the Grace of Our Father shall We go forth as mighty warriors - that there be Greater knowledge amongst them which now walk in flesh - - let them seek the Light - and feign not wisdom --

Let the Light pour forth - let them see - let them hear - and walk upright - knowing whither they are bound --

So be it profitable unto them -- Amen and Selah --

See the hand of God move - and ye shall Know that it moves with precision - for it errors not in its movement -- Give unto Me credit for Knowing that which I say and do - for it is given unto Me to Know - - and blest are they which KNOW -- So be it that I shall reveal unto them which follow Me - many new and marvellous wonders -- So let it suffice thee that I Am Come that ye might Know --

For this do We of the Host go forth - that "they" be quickened into the Greater Life - the Greater part - that they come into the fullness of their estate -- For man hast not as yet come into the fullness of his inheritance - he is not as yet accountable for himself - he is as yet immature -- Therefore We come at this time that he might become aware of his inheritance - and be up and about his new part - - for it is now come when he shall move forward - into greater fields - greater glories --

This is our part - to assist him in his movement forward - not as his poor puny priest - to give unto him a new religion - a new philosophy - new sayings - signs and wonders -- While he looks for signs and wonders - We say it is the lesser part - - We are concerned with the Greater - and for this do We say: "As ye are prepared so shall ye receive" - "be ye not concerned with the trivialities" - these are detriments and stumbling blocks --

Consider well that which is said - and be ye as one thotful of that which is said - - let thine mind be staid on the Source of thine BEing - and give credit where credit is due --

Bless thyself in the doing - and be ye as one prepared for to receive of the Greater Glories -- Hast it not been said: Ye shall worship only The Father - The Cause of thy Being -- Wherein hast thou bowed before the altars of the poor priests which hast set himself up - that he glorify himself?

Hast thou given credit where credit is due? Hast thou put thine hand in thy pocket - that I be assisted in Mine Work? Hast thou gone the last mile with Me? Hast thou given unto the ones which ask of Me assistance? Hast thou placed within their path a stumbling block? Hast thou spoken evil of Mine Associates - Mine devoted Servants? Hast thou paid homage unto them? Hast thou given unto them due respect - support - a helping hand?

Wherein hast thou called thyself "Good" - blameless - - wherein hast thou set thyself up as judge of Mine Servants - Mine Associates - members of Mine Household?

I beg of thee - consider well that which I have said - and be ye as one on whose shoulders rests the great responsibility of thine own preparation for the Greater part -- So be it and Selah --

To them which seek the Light I would speak -- To them which are prepared to forsake all to follow the Light I would say: Put aside all thy petty notions of The Father The Source of thy BEing - thy preconceived ideas of The Son of God - Sent of Him The Father - and be ye as one prepared to enter into the Light - the Light which never fails --

By thy own puny ideas art thou bound - for it is given unto Me to Know - for I see the great darkness which hast covered thee - the gross darkness of men's ignorance of the Light - and wherein he is bound -- Let thine bondage be broken - let thine own light shine forth - and ye shall be as one prepared to enter into the Greater Glories --

Fear not that which ye know not - - fear that which ye know - that binds thee -- It is said: "The wages of sin is death"- it is so - for the ignorance of man is his sin - and that which he knows - and which he clings to is his undoing - his infraction of the law -- To know that which binds thee and cling unto it is of the dark - "sin" - and it behooves thee to know that which is of the Light -- Therefore a Host passes amongst thee - and the cry hast gone forth: "Come ye out of darkness - - be ye as one alert - awaken ye - and come forth as one alive" --

Hear ye - and respond unto the cry - and be ye as one lifted up --

This is the Word I bring unto thee this day -- Bless thyself to see the hand of God move - - see it move - and be ye as one prepared to accept that which is proffered unto thee -- Put thine hand forth and receive that which is proffered thee - for the Host stands by to assist thee in thine time of preparation -- Be ye as one blest by Me - for I Am One of the Host -- So be it and Selah -- The time is come for the voice in the Wilderness to be heard - and heard it shall be - for the Host makes strait-way that it be so - so shall it be --

Be ye as one which hast ears - and let the Voice ring out - and let it be heard by all: "This is the Voice crying in the Wilderness"--

And it is given unto Me to go before the Mighty Shining One - which is the Host of the Host - and whose shoes I am unworthy to tie - - yet I am with Him - I am upon His right hand - for I am His hand made manifest - and I say unto thee: I am His Will - even as He is The Father's Will --

I come at His behest - I go at His behest - and I am His Servant indeed - for I serve with Mine whole being - wholeheartedly - without reservation -- I ask nothing more than the joy of serving - - I give of myself that the way be made strait before Him - The Shining One --

The Glory is His - - I am but the One walking with Him - for He is the One to Whom I bow in humble contrition - in submission unto the Will of The Father which hast brot us forth - that We might be as His hand made manifest before All men -- This is the day for which We have waited - and for which We have worked -- So let it profit them which have the will to follow where He leads - for He hast been unto us the Wayshower - and We have followed gladly and willingly -- Now We find that We have been guided aright - and the joy which We share no man knows - until it hast been his by experience --

This is the experience allotted unto every man which follows in His footsteps -- So be it that I am but One which stands by - as One with Him - as One of the Host -- There are many - uncounted are they - which are now assigned the task of passing amongst "them" which sleepeth - that they be quickened - awakened - that they come forth prepared to receive their inheritance in full -- So be it and Selah -- This is Mine Word unto thee at this hour -- So be it that I shall speak at another hour --

Recorded by Sister Thedra

The Highest = Solen Aum Solen

Sori Sori -- There are none so Great as The One Which is called Solen Aum Solen -- Forever is He the Greater - forever is He above Us the Sons -- There are none which equal Him - for He is the First and the Last - The Eternal Father - the Cause of Our Being --

There is none above Him - as We Know Him to be the Highest - the Supreme over All - the Beginning and the End -- from Him We went forth - unto Him We return --

This is the part which hast been shown unto Us - for it is with this Knowledge that We go forth to bear witness of Him -- There are no words - no pen - which can convey the Grandeur of His Place of Abode -- There is no joy known unto man which equals the joy of them which are gathered therein - - and for this is it said: "Come - See" - and Know ye that it is Greater than thou hast seen - or imaged --

There are no words which human tongue can find - to convey one iota of the Beauty - Grandeur - Glory which pervades the place of His Abode -- None have brot with them such Knowledge - yet they have been as ones prepared to enter in - - they are as ones prepared ere they enter - for none other may enter --

So be it that I speak from out of the Holy of Holies - wherein they are gathered for the Greater Part - wherein they are come for the Great occasion of receiving One which cometh unto Us from out another Realm - wherein they are prepared to come unto Us --

Some come singly - some come in concert - many come - and the many or singly are received as the One and Only Son of God - there are no distinctions - each is given the Special Part - and each His place - and He is given the Honor and respect of all others regardless of number - - each hast his place reserved for him - and he answers unto his name and number --

The music sounds - and many trumpeters stand at attention signifying His entrance -- The Colors are raised - and the Host appears - and stands before them - or before him - which hast come into this place -- The Host raises His hand in Holy Benediction - and places it upon the head of this newly arrived One - which kneels before Him to receive His blessing --

The choir bursts forth with the anthem: "Hail! Hail! a Son is risen this day - Hail - Hail unto the New born Son - Hail unto the King - the King of Kings" --

Blest are they which receive their Sonship -- So be it and Selah --

This is but part of the Great and Glorious Scene - as it is now being enacted within the place wherein I am - and this is but the beginning of a Great and lengthy part which I shall be priveleged to speak of -- So be it I shall give unto thee another part - and ye shall receive it in the Name of The Most High God -- So be it and Selah --

Talents

Sori Sori -- To thee I would say: Hide not thine talents - for there is yet greater to be added - - and for that matter greater things to be revealed unto thee -- Discount not thine own part - and put thine part with Mine - and together shall they be placed within the record as one account -- Ye shall be as one responsible for thine own - - I shall be responsible for Mine - yet together they shall be put within the records - for them which are to follow - - so let it profit them to know which is given unto thee -- This is Mine word at this time -- So be it and Selah --

Pray ye that they betray not themself - for they shall stand as ones accountable for themselves - and they shall be held accountable for that which they do with the Word -- Now it is said that many shall awaken - it is so - - yet many shall be as ones which awaken - and then they shall fall by the wayside as ones which have not the will to go forward - as ones prepared for to enter into the "Holy of Holies"--

These shall be as ones which weary of the way in which - I lead them - - these shall turn from the strait and narrow - and look for the things which they delight in - and find their own fortune hast been pilfered from them by the deceiver - which hast betrayed them --

= **Character** =

These are to be pitied - for they have not the strength of character to endure the puny and agonizing temptations - the scorn of their fellow men - the temptation they set before them - that which is designed to trip them up -- These are the ones which think themself wise - yet they know not that which they shall find before them - when they stand face to face with themself -- So be it that I Know - for I see them crying out for assistance - and in shame they cry for assistance --

Therefore it is said: "Betray not thyself - for there are none so sad" -- So be it I see them as ones in shame - in disgrace - despised of men and lost - as ones lost! - and wandering they know not where - - these are the ones which heed not that which is said - and the ones which turn aside - as the ones which betray themself - these are the pitiful ones - lost! lost! I say! - these are in darkness --

The ones which have betrayed their trust shall be as ones fortuned the days in darkness - allotted unto them - when they shall again come to know that there are none so sad as the ones which betray his trust - or himself --

These are the ones which shall give of themself that they become accountable for themself - their every act/ deed/ word/ thot -- So be it they shall rectify their deeds of darkness - and they shall turn from them

- and go into the next place as ones prepared - cleansed - renewed - made new -- So be it and Selah --

The Way of the Lord

Sori Sori -- For this hour let us speak of the Way of the Lord - the Way in which He would lead us - thee - them which would be led by Him - -

He hast Come from out the Realm of Light - that He might give the ones in darkness freedom - - it is offered unto them that they be lifted up - that they might know eternal freedom --

The price is obedience unto the law - acceptance of thy own responsibility -- This is All that is asked of them which seek their freedom -- The Way is before them - and it is the Way unto The Father's House - the place wherein He hast prepared for them which are prepared to enter in - - it is the place wherein there is no sorrow - no darkness - - therein is joy - and everlasting Peace - Peace they have not known --

The Peace which I speak of is Eternal - and the Light is the Eternal Light from which All Peace cometh -- Let it be thine part to seek and to find - - so be it that ye shall not be denied - for the Host stands ready to serve thee - and to be unto thee thine servant - in the Way The Father would have them serve -- So be it that the Way is strait before thee - and none shall say thee "Nay" - for it is given unto thee to choose which way ye go -- So be it that the Way of The Lord is before each and every man - and it is Our part to show him in which direction he should go - -

= **The Part of the Host** =

Let it be understood that the part of the Host is to do that which is given unto Us - for We are too under a law - not unlike the child of Earth - yet not the same law - for Our law which binds Us is the Law of Love -- We serve Him because of Our Love - the Love of Righteousness - and when We see the joy - peace - and freedom which is Ours - We turn and give unto him a glad hand - that he too might come to Know as We - for there is none within this place wherein I am - which hast not known the joy of freedom - and the sorrow which is given unto man - for man hast not the mind to remember the joy which he forfeited - when he took upon himself the body of "flesh" --

This is the way of flesh - to forget the way of sorrow - darkness - - sad is his plight -- This is the Word I would speak this hour - - let him be as one lifted up - let him know the joy which is Ours - the Joy of the Victor -- Let him praise the Name of Solen Aum Solen - for His Grace - and Mercy - for it is by dis Grace and Mercy that We - the Host - are assembled for the purpose of bringing them out of bondage --

Let thy time be the time of preparation - for Greater Glories await thee -- Praise ye The Father - Praise ye the Name of Solen - and with thine Whole Being - for it is with thy Being that He is praised - honored -- Thy word is but a mockery without thy self surrender - selfless surrender - - no thot of self - save for Him - His Work - - His Work shall be thine - and ye shall be directed with Love and Wisdom -- So let it profit thee ---

Permission Granted by the Council

Sori Sori -- This is Our time - the time for Our communication - and it is with great joy that I speak - for I come as Mine Associates - with the consent of The Council - thru which it is necessary to pass - - therefore I am come even as the others - by the consent of The Council - which hast given Us permission --

The Permission is necessary for the Work which is given Us to do - - the Work allotted Us is given according to law - and by the same law are We required to appear before the Council - that We might be approved -- It is said: "Many are called and few are chosen" - so it is here - - many would speak - or ask that they come unto thee - - yet as a member of The Host - I say unto thee in great humility - that none are allowed to come unto thee without consent of The Host - for it is by Their consent that each hast come - and that each hast spoken - - for this have They been blest - for this hast thou been blest - for it is a part of the Plan that each be prepared for a part which is yet unrevealed - which is far greater than ye have dreamed --

The Way in which it shall be revealed is strange unto thee - and new unto All - - while it shall be most efficient it is new - and strange -- Therefore it shall be as the Light - revealed gently as thou canst bear it - and ye shall be as one prepared to receive the fullness of the Plan - for ye shall grow in strength and Knowledge - then ye shall be as one firm of foot - and there shall be no fear - no shocks --

This is but the beginning - and the part which ye have is no small part - yet ye discount thine own part -- I say unto thee: Be ye not as the one which doubts his own part or capability - the talent is but buried beneath a scarf -- Be ye as one which hast buried it - and lift it from the scarf - and look ye well upon it - and be ye glad for thine own talent - and bless it - nourish it - and see it grow -- So be it and Selah --

Profitable Service

Sori Sori - Hear Me in this - and be ye as one prepared for yet Greater things -- This is the Word I bring unto thee: This is the day in which The Host goes forth in full power - and in the Power which is given unto Us of The Father - - We shall do that which is necessary to awaken the sleepers --

The ones which are prepared to come forth - shall be brot out in Great Glory - - Great numbers shall be brot out - and likewise - great numbers shall be left - - these shall be as the ones which are unprepared - these shall find they are wanting - they shall be put into a place wherein they shall prepare themself for the "Greater Part"--

This is the Word I would give unto them which have begun to stir:

Be ye about thy preparation - let thine hand be turned to service which would profit thee - Service unto mankind -- There is wisdom in Service - yet there is Wisdom in Knowing how - and when to serve -- To serve well is to lift up thy fellow man - - add not unto his deficiency - add not unto his slothfulness - put not thine hand into the pocket of another to give unto the laggard - the slothful - - lift him up - let him stand on his own feet - teach him to stand with head high and feet firmly fixt --

= Responsibility =

Let him carry his own weight - and drag not his feet -- Let him be his own servant - ask not of him that which he cannot do - - yet - he shall do that which he is capable of - for his potentials shall be brot out - <u>and increased</u> --

So be it I say: Ye shall serve wisely - - let them multiply their own talents - gifts - and let them know the joy of serving - for this is the joy of the <u>Initiate</u> -- We serve gladly - that others might be brot out of their lethargy and darkness - that others might Know the joy of serving selflessly -- So be it and Selah --

While it is said - "ye shall serve selflessly"- it is also said: "Ye shall serve with wisdom" - for there are ones which would ride thy back - and the load should be more than thou couldst bear - therein would be no profit unto either -- While it is given unto thee to stand on Higher Ground - ye may lift them up - - yet - should they pull thee down - both should flounder in the ditch --

Give with wisdom - serve with wisdom - and fret not for them which have not the mind <u>to be lifted up</u> -- Give unto them as they are prepared to receive - no more - for to choke them is of no service -- Let them assimilate that which is given - then they shall have another portion - and then they shall assimilate it before another - - therein they shall be as one prepared for the next - without the discomfort of "indigestion" --

These which are prone to read the letter of the Word - and then rush out crying: Fraud - fraud - are not ready to serve Me - Life - Light - neither their fellowman -- So be it that these shall be the traitors - and they shall wait their time -- So be it they shall cry for assistance - that they might assist others - for they shall Know the sorrow of waiting - the sadness of betrayal -- So be it and Selah --

The Guardians

Sori Sori -- Behold! the Way before thee - and be ye as one blest to enter therein -- It is come when ye shall be fortuned to walk with them which keep watch - them which have been given charge over thee --

These are but thy Benefactors - the Ones to Whom thou art (aware) forever thankful - - and ye shall be as one prepared to walk with Them and counsel with Them -- So be it and Selah --

These are but thy Porters - thy Benefactors - which stand guard - and which have gone before thee that the way be prepared before thee -- These are the Ones which keep watch - and They bear testimony of thee - They bear witness of thee thy going and coming -- They have no thot of reward - save thine own part which is fortuned unto thee for the Good of All -- For that do They come - They draw nigh that the Father's Will be done - - so shall it be - for it is so decreed -- So let it be --

The Way - The Law

Sori Sori - The time is now come when We shall bring forth a new part - which shall be new and strange unto "them" - - they shall be as ones stricken with awe <u>and</u> fright - for they shall have no fore-knowledge of that which shall be done --

There are some which will have no knowledge of that which is BEING done while they go about their puny affairs--

I say - they see not the Plan - not even in part -- It is given unto Me to see the Whole of the Plan - while ye see but in minute part - - it is for this that I say: Come up higher - that ye might see in greater measure --

The part which is given unto Me is to direct them which are of a mind to come up higher - to go all the way with Me - - and for this do I work without ceasing -- So be it and Selah --

I say unto thee: Look! See! Watch! the hand of God Move - - as a mighty pendulum doth it swing - - as a Mighty Hand doth it move to and fro over the land - over the seas -- Thru the Cosmos it moves! - and it is given unto Me to see the movements thereof --

There is nothing hidden from Me - for I Am One with the Plan - and I bring forth the fulfillment of it - concerning the Earth and the inhabitants thereof -- I bring forth the Great Laws concerning the Earth and the fullness thereof -- I give unto thee the law - and ye but do thy part in the fulfilling thereof - inasmuch as it concerns thee -- So be it that it concerns thee not - that which others do - - be ye as one concerned of thine own part - thine own way - Hear YE that which I say - and prepare thyself for thy new part - and ye shall not fail --

This is the Way - the Truth - and the Law provides thee time and a place for thy preparation - ye have but to apply the Law -- And be ye not anxious for thine Victory - thine own welfare - for ye shall be provided - as thou art prepared -- So be it and Selah --

Honor the Father

Sori Sori -- Mine Word unto them which seek the Light shall be: Bring thyself in full surrender - Wholly surrender - that The Father might use thy hands - thy feet - to do His Work/ His Will - for has He not endowed unto thee thine being?

Thou hast been given Life - of His Life - why deny Him that which is His? Put thine own self within His hand - and fear nought - for He is thy Father first and last - - He Knows thee for that which thou art - and therein is thy strength - - bear ye witness of Him - Honor The Father - Glorify His Name - make no mockery of it - bless thyself in so doing--

Walk ye with surety - and be ye steadfast in thine work - in thy worship - and be ye blest -- So be it I speak as One of The Host - - therein is the Authority with which I speak - for I have gone the way in which ye are directed - therefore I speak as One with Authority -- And it is the first time that I have spoken - and it is given unto Me to be prepared to speak again - - for the Good of all shall I speak --

It is given unto Me to stand with the Shining One Which hast given unto Me passport - that I might enter into the vibration of flesh - for it is long since I left the vibration of flesh - - long have I been preparing for this hours - when I might enter into such activities - that which shall be much Light unto the ones groping in darkness -- The way is now clear when I might step thru the barrier - and speak as One which hast won Mine Victory --

It is not the easy way - it is the safe way - and none wherein I am have won their Victory without the labor of Love - long weary miles of searching - of work - toil - heartache and share - for I say - the denial is shame - and it wast given unto Me to deny the Truth - the Light - the Christ - and for that I felt such shame as ye shall not know -- Pray for them which deny The Christ! It is He Which is known as The Shining One Which stands by - that We have seen - and know that He is The Christ - The Host of The Host --

There are ones which deny Him - that know Him not - - these shall come to know - and they shall be blest -- It is given unto Us to Know Him as He is -- It is said: "Ye shall put from thee all thy preconceived ideas of and about Him"- it is so - for to Know Him is to rejoice and be glad - - for this I wish to share with thee Mine Greatest Joy -- So be it I shall speak again and again - as it is expedient -- So be it and Selah - -

The Coming

Sori Sori -- Let us speak of the coming - "The Coming" so often referred to by the ones which have little knowledge of the meaning of "The Coming" -- Many speak so lightly of "The Coming" of which they know nothing --

They speak of the COMING as tho they Knew the meaning - - it is not the way they image --

They speak of the Coming in Great Glory as tho it would be with Great Pomp and Ceremony - - it is not the way they have imaged --

They speak of the Coming in a cloud - they have imaged a vain image - for they are the ones in the cloud! - the cloud is of their making - - yet they shall see that "He" is Come with His Host -- While it is not as they have imaged - they shall see that He is Come - that it is not as they expected - - for this many shall go into the next place which is prepared for them - knowing not that He is Come this day bringing with Him His Mighty Host --

These which go out of the realm of flesh knowing not - shall be schooled in the place wherein they are put - and they shall find that they have / on the subject which they did not accept while in flesh --

These shall be as ones quickened - and they shall know - and be as ones prepared to return - that they too - might assist in the resurrection --

Now consider well that which is said - - there are ones which have not accepted the "WORD"- these shall find a place prepared for them - wherein they shall learn - - their progression is certain - they shall progress - some slowly - some swiftly - yet none shall be overlooked - none neglected - - each shall be put in his proper place - and each shall have the necessary assistance --

= Patience =

There are ones which have been enlightened - and turned aside in despair -- These shall find themself in another "place" wherein they shall see the wisdom of patience - - and these shall see that they have been untrue to themself --

= The Victors =

Now - while these have found their proper places - there are others which have heard the Word - heeded - followed in the way set before them - - they have endured the trials - temptations - and held fast - -

these shall find they have overcome - and they shall be hailed as the Victors - they shall be received as the Victors -- So be it they shall Know the meaning of "The Coming in Great Glory" - for these shall be the ones prepared - - the ones quickened shall see - and hear -- So be it and Selah --

Wait not for signs and miracles - great mysterious wonders - for He is Come in Great Power - and in Glory -- Give unto The Father Praise and the Glory - for the Power and the Glory is HIS!! --

Seek ye the Light and it shall be revealed -- Ask of no man his opinion - for it is given unto man to be walking in "the cloud" - - a dark cloud it is - not of dust - not of smoke - - We see it as a dense fog -- Floundering is he - he sees not his way - - pity is he - pity is the one which hast not heard - accepted - followed the "Word" - seen the Light --

These are the ones which stumble over the WORD - and see not -- These are the ones which cry for assistance - knowing not it is at hand -- These are the ones which deny that He is Come - that the day of Salvation is at hand -- So be it I say unto them: "Come ye higher - See the Glory of The Lord - for He is Come" -- So be it and Selah --

The Keeper of the Records

Sori Sori -- Be ye as one on whose head I place Mine hand - and ye shall be blest of Me and by Me -- So be it and Selah --

I hold within Mine hand the record of thy sojourn within the realm of flesh -- I too see thy record from thy journey thru the Cosmos - for hast thou not traveled far - - thou hast not just begun thy travels -- It is Mine part to Know the way ye have gone - the time of thy going - the time of thy return -- So be it I am the Keeper of the Records - and for this am I prepared to speak of "The Records" which thou hast made - and which I have kept --

The Keeper of the Records hast no responsibility for the record made - he is responsible for the Keeping thereof -- So be it that as ye keep the record within the "Gate House"- so do I keep the records within the place wherein I am --

I am a "Keeper of the Records" even as thou art - and it behooves thee to know that each record is part of the Whole - each piece a part of the Whole - - and the time swiftly approaches when all the pieces shall be placed together as One - and it is given unto Me to see it as One - with no parts missing --

Yet there shall come One - which shall be as one on whose shoulders rests the responsibility of putting the pieces together - and then he shall be as one which hast gone a long way - for his part shall be as one of great importance - great import -- When he hast set himself to the task of putting all the pieces together - he shall find that there are Greater things to be learned from the pieces than he had imaged --

He shall be as one greatly blest - for he shall come to know the true from the false - - he shall come to know that from the ashes come Greater Mansions -- So be it he shall ponder Mine Words - and he shall learn much from them - - he shall be as one prepared for the Greater revelation -- So be it it shall profit him --

I Am Ishmael

The Affairs of Man

Sori Sori -- Mine Word I would give unto thee this hour - is:- By the time they find this Word they shall see a change in the affairs of men - for the affairs of men shall be as never before - they shall be as ones concerned with the part of food - and life - for life within flesh depends upon food - and this is the pity of it -- The puny part of food is the part which they give unto man - - they are wont to improve upon Nature - and this is the poor part of wisdom -- They classify each and every unit of food - and give it names and numbers - and they put within it the poor additives - and they call it "enriched" - how so - is it enriched? By what means is it enriched?

This is the poor part of food - it is said it is given unto the physical part of man to need food - food of the Earth - the substance of the Earth from which it cometh -- Yet the Earth hast provided within the natural growth - the needed substance for the body - the physical body of man -- It is said: "Make no fetish of food"- eat that which cometh from the Earth - and adulterate it not - - the part which is added to - or taken away is of no account - yet ye shall remember that it is given unto the physical body to eat of the elements which are of Earthly substance - that of the herbs - grain - and the fruit thereof --

While the strong animal is but the larger for the being animal which he is - he is not the larger for the eating - for his part is that of animal - not man -- The oxen is the oxen - man is man - and he hast the same flesh - yet of different blood -- He hast not the same blood - the same protosphere -- Therefore man is not the beast - neither hast he the blood of the beast - - he is the one set apart as man - and for this he shall refrain from consuming the flesh and blood of the animal -- So be it the better part of wisdom --

Many Stations - On the Path

Sori Sori -- Mighty - Mighty is the hand of God - - see it move - and know ye that ye see - and Know that ye Know -- Be ye not dismayed - for I say unto thee: I am with thee - and I am thy Shield and thy Buckler --

I bring unto thee One which hast not spoken - - this is new unto him - yet he hast proven himself - and I have placed upon him Mine Seal - and ye shall accept him in Mine Name - for I am as One responsible for him -- This I say unto thee at this hour --

(Dawn) Be ye blest to receive Me - for I come as permitted by the Council - and I say unto thee: Many stand with Me that there be Light and strength within thy realm -- I am now One prepared to put forth Mine hand for the healing of man - the world of man -- Yet it is for this that The Host is gathered in One body - as One Man - - for this do We speak with One Voice --

There is but One Lord God - and He is The Shining One - The One to Whom We are accountable - to Whom We give accounting --

He asks of Us nought save that We obey the law set forth - and that We do that which is given unto Us to do -- This is Our part at present: To go forth that We might assist them which seek the Light -- The Light never fails - yet there are many within the realms of flesh which seek the Light for a time - then weary - faint and fall by the way - - this We see - this We Know - this We would do: Be unto them the strength needed to gain the summit - to go forward unto the top --

The path - steep and rugged - is strait and narrow - therefore We stoop to offer Our assistance - that they might not fall - nor error -- For

The Way is clearly marked - and there are ones stationed on the way - along the way - to assist as is needful -- And it is Mine part to be prepared to take up My station on a place wherein many shall pass as weary travelers - desolate - disconsolate - disillusioned - and weak -- I say it is Mine part to give unto them strength and comfort - that they press on toward the Goal -- Yet I see them fall to the left - to the right - yet the many pass - and are prepared to enter into the place wherein there is no failure --

I say "Failure"- - while I see <u>their</u> failure - I see them as resting - and that which is failure shall become their strength - for they shall grow in strength - strength of Spirit - strength of character - - and they shall awaken unto their own potentials - they shall mature - and be glad for their strength -- So be it that I am but One stationed along the path - that they be safe - that they be brot out of their deep sleep - their lethargy -- So be it I Am One of The Host --

The Head of this House

Sori Sori -- This is Mine Word unto thee: Bless them which misuse thee - keep thy own council - keep thine own way - for thou hast chosen the Way of The Lord - - let not thy foot slip - answer them not! Give the enemy no footing -- It is said: "If ye are not with Me ye are against Me"- it is so - - so be it with thee - - they are with thee or against thee - for none serve two masters -- This is the House of The Lord - set upon the sure foundation - I have declared it so - so let it suffice thee -- Give unto them no room - no footing - - provide for them no comfort - let them go their way in peace - and find their own way - hard tho it be --

Give unto them nothing which they can put into their pockets - which they can pilfer --

Guard well thy door - let not the dragon rest upon it - in wait for a pennys worth of food in which to delight --

Be ye steadfast - and fret not for them which would but trip thee up -- It is said: "I am thy Shield and thy Buckler" - I stand at the portal - I am the Keeper of this House - and I forsake not Mine servants - - Mine Servants Know Me and serve Me - therefore We are One - - so be it a House United - and in unity there is Strength --

So let it be - - Amen and Selah -- -

Great Discoveries - Revelations

Sori Sori -- Be ye blest this hour - this is the time for Me to say: "This is Our time - the time for Our communication" be ye as one blest - for I come that ye be blest -- So let it be --

This is the day of Great revelation - Great things shall be revealed in a short while - and this is but the beginning - this is but the beginning! While it is the beginning - the Greater is not so far distant --

Man shall stand in amazement and awe - for he shall see that which is beyond his comprehension -- He hast not dreamed of such wonders - - and for this hast it been said: They shall stand in awe and amazement -- For he hast thot himself wise - that he hast been within the time of great fulfillment - yet it is said: He is as yet immature - and he shall fine that he hast but begun his learning - that he is not finished - that he hast not found the end of all things!

So be it that the way is now open for the Greater learning - and there shall be Great and Wonderful manifestations which he hast not dreamed of - for there is come into thy midst - some which are prepared to bring forth these manifestations which shall be for the Good of All mankind - so let it be -- I say unto thee: "Watch - Look! See - and Know - for it is recorded that One shall send forth a Mighty Host which shall lift man - which shall be Great Light unto him - and it shall be for the Good of the generations yet unborn -- So be it and Selah --

While I say - it shall be for the generations unborn - I too say: Ye shall see that which shall be done - and ye shall be glad -- So be it and Selah --

Recorded by Sister Thedra

Choose Wisely

Sori Sori -- Be ye as one on whose head I lay Mine hand - and ye shall be blest of Me and by Me -- This is Mine Word unto them which are of a mind to follow Me:--

The Way is prepared - I have gone before thee - I have given unto thee the Law - - now I am Come - with a Mighty Host - and it shall be as the forerunner of Me - - the Ones of the Host shall go forth - and each One shall do that which is given unto him to do - none shall fail - - While others (of flesh) shall fail - none of the Host shall fail - for their part is to do that which is allotted unto them - - when this is accomplished - they shall not be held accountable for the part of the ones which fail in their part --

The part which is given unto the ones in the physical realm - is to alert themself to the Presence of The Host - and accept that which they bring for their enlightenment --

These which accept - and follow to the end - shall find they have chosen wisely - they shall find they have made their choice freely and wisely -- None shall carry them upon their back - none shall bring them against their will --

There are ones which shall hear - and reject that which they hear - - others shall hear and put not forth their hand to assist themself - for fear of being deceived --

= Alter Ego =

Others shall be deceived by their own selfish desire - - these shall image the vain imaging - and "they" shall make for themself great and fancy images - and portray themself as great heroes and martyrs - and great beauties - and gladiators -- These shall go out as the emissaries of their own altars - and declare themself <u>So</u> and <u>So</u> - - -

These shall find that they have tript themself up - and they shall be as ones bound by their own foolishness --

= Admonition =

Now it is said: "'Come ye forth as a little child - in humility - and ye shall be as one led - and ye shall be as one directed in the way of the righteous -- Fear not - yet ye shall not set thyself up - ye shall be as one alert - and follow ye the Light - and ye shall not fall"--

The ones which seek the Light shall be found and led gently - led as little children - as ones fortuned to be the chosen - the ones which have surrendered themself unto the Light -- These shall be dealt with gently and wisely - - therefore they shall find that there are no places they can hide - no place they can be lost from sight - they shall be as ones protected - guided and sheltered in the time of storm -- So be it and Selah --

Blest are the ones which follow where I lead them - for they shall not want -- Sananda hast spoken this day -- So be it and Selah --

The Way of the Initiate

Sori Sori -- This is Mine Word for this hour: The Way for the Initiate is clearly recorded - and it is given unto thee to Know - for hast thou not recorded it - and hast it not been said before: "The Way of the Initiate is the Way of Truth and Justice" -- So be it the Initiate walks the Way in which he should go - the way I point - the way I lead - and none weary of the Word/ of the Work given unto them to do --

This is the Way of initiation:- Work - Dedication - Obedience unto the law - - and then the accomplishment is the reward -- So be it that Service is the Work which is given unto them which aspire to the attaining to the   -- Let it profit them to obey the law - and to be as the humble - and obedient soldier - "Soldiers of The Cross" - these shall attain -- So be it and Selah --

The Measure of Time

Sori Sori -- Bless this day - bless thyself - be ye as one blest to receive Me - for it is now come when great shall be thy revelation - - Great shall be thy Revelation! Let it be for the Good of All - for it is given unto Me to see the Work as done - therefore I Know - I Know that which shall be accomplished --

For this can I speak with Authority -- I measure not time by the hours - nor the days - nor the years -- I say I do not measure time by the years - - I measure time by events -- That which is to be done - shall be done within the time allotted unto such Work - then it shall be as finished - and I shall go - even as I came - and the Book shall be closed - for I shall be as One finished - as One which hast done Mine part - and taken Mine leave - - then another shall fill Mine place - Mine Office - and He shall do His part - even as I did Mine part --

I say: When Mine Work is finished - I shall take with Me Mine own - them which have followed Me - and these shall go where I go - and they shall be as I - free and without guilt or blemish - for they shall be as ones prepared to enter into the place wherein I am - - they shall be as ones prepared to go with Me where I go -- So be it and Selah --

Be ye as One blest to go all the way with Me -- So be it and Selah --

Friend & Enemy

Sori Sori-- Hast it not been said that there are ones which would be unto thee thy Shield and they Buckler - it is so - - and there are ones which would be thine undoing - which would beset thee - usurp thine time - thine energy - pick thy pockets and turn thee out -- So be it that I am not of a mind to give unto them comfort - - I am not of a mind to give unto them aught -- So be it I withdraw Mine hand - and they shall find their way -- So be it and Selah --

I am now prepared to see this thru - - however - ye know not that which I say - neither do ye know that which they do - or say - which is designed to belittle thee -- So be it that I Know that which goes on - and it behooves Me to forestall that which they <u>think</u> to do - for I shall be unto them their Porter - they shall not pass - neither shall they put their foot against thee -- Such is Mine Word unto thee this day -- Be ye alert - fear not - heed ye that which I say unto thee - and be ye as one blest --

So be it and Selah --

Assurance

Sori Sori -- By Mine hand shall ye be led into fields afar - and therein ye shall find wonders untold - therein ye shall find the joy of Serving the Light - as the Ones which have gone before thee - - for They shall be gathered together as One Body - One Mighty Host - and there shall be no sorrow --

Blest are they which come into the place wherein I am - - they shall be as One with Me - and it shall be the time of Work and rejoicing - for We shall see the fruits of Our labors -- Be ye as One with Me - and rejoice forevermore -- So be it a glad day --

Revelation:- "In the Freedom of Spirit" - (Thedra)

The scene opens as I stand inside a great hall - I remembered it as a "Masonic Hall" - it had not been in use for some time - - now it is being prepared for use - - I had waited for this -- On the opposite side of the hall stood a long table - - the floor of wood - highly polished - needed cleaning -- In the hall outside the door - stood a group of people representing all countries -- They wore their native costumes - they were waiting for the Hall to be prepared -- I had waited for the "Master Carpenter" to affix the Master's Chair to the wall - or in its place - - I found it had been done - - I said: "I am glad that is done" -- I turned to a young lad - who had refused to do an errand assigned to him - - I asked him: "How is your art of polishing floors?" He said: "I think I can do that" --

The Resurrection

Sori Sori -- This I would say unto thee this day: There are ones which have the Power and the Authority to bring thee out of bondage - - yet it is given unto These to be prepared for the part given unto Them - - to find the ones which are prepared - and to bring them out - to bring them in as the harvest*- as the ones of the fold -- So be it that I am the Shepherd of the fold - and it behooves Me to bring in the ones which are now prepared --

So be it that I say unto thee: Stand ye ready to assist them which is given unto thy keeping - - so be it that they shall be as ones responsible for that which they do with that which ye give unto them -- So be it and Selah -- Fret not for their unknowing - for their behavior - - put within their hands the Word - and direct them aright - and therein thy responsibility ends - - for this hast it been said: Give unto them which ask - and unto them that which they can assimilate - choke them not - for they are as the babe as yet -- Let them grow - let them expand their minds that they might comprehend that which is said unto them -- So be it that they shall receive as they are prepared -- So be it and Selah - -

*Beloved Sananda: Is this what is called the Resurrection - which You refer to as the harvest?

Indeed it is the harvest - yet it is the Resurrection -- Each age hast a Resurrection - and it is said: When this one is complete - I shall withdraw for a time - and then they shall labor long and hard while they wait for the next -- So be it and Selah --

The Anointment

Sori Sori -- Such is the Way of The Lord - such is the Word of The Lord: The Way of Obedience - Dedication - Application of the law -- The Word is applied unto thyself - and ye dedicate thyself to the law - and none say unto thee otherwise - for thou hast heard them not -- Thou hast obeyed and followed where I have pointed - where I have gone ye shall go - and there shall be no more mysteries -- Ye shall set upon Mine right hand - and I shall anoint thee with sweet oil -- So be it and Selah --

Direction

Sori Sori -- Be ye as one on whose head I place Mine hand in Holy Benediction - and ye shall be blest of Me and by Me -- Be ye as one responsible for that which ye do with the Word I give unto thee - and ye shall be as one called to Greater Work - - Greater things shall be given unto thee to do - for ye shall go into far fields - wherein ye shall find many strange and wonderful things - New things - New Revelations - which ye shall give unto them which are prepared to receive -- So be it that "they" shall be as ones prepared - and ye shall do that which is given unto thee to do - and they shall do "their" part --

It is said: "Ye shall do that which I do - ye shall go where I go"- it is so - for this art thou now prepared -- Ye shall walk with Me - and counsel with Me - for the Good of All shall it be -- Ye shall see and Know - as I Know - ye shall walk Knowingly - - ye shall not fail - for Mine hand shall be upon thee -- So be it and Selah --

Prophesy

Sori Sori --Lo - I say unto thee this day: The time cometh swiftly when there shall be Greater tribulations - Greater anxiety upon the land - and the seas - - the seas shall give up her Secrets - the land shall not bring forth the supply necessary for their needs -- The harvests shall fail - the people shall cry for food - they shall find themself without shelter - without food! - and they shall find that pestilence shall overrun the land - for they have not been as good custodians of that which hast been given into their keeping -- They have been as the traitors - and the poor in spirit - they have turned a deaf ear unto Mine Word - they have heeded not --

Now the day of reckoning is come - when they shall cry: "Lord! Lord! how much longer" --

This is the Word I would give unto thee at this hour -- Ye shall add that which ye will - and it shall profit them to heed that which is said - - So be it and Selah --

This is the time for which I have waited - the time wherein they shall be as ones prepared to accept the hand proffered them --

So be it I Am Come that All men might be lifted up - yet they reject Me - Mine Word - Mine Servants -- So let them profit by the lesson learned - - I Am Come that they might learn - and Know - the Way of Truth and Justice -- So be it and Selah --

Flesh vs Spirit

Sori Sori -- For this hour let us speak of the Spirit which animates flesh - the physical body - that which is called "man" --

The "man" is not physical -- Flesh is flesh - and Man is the pounder - he hast the Spirit -- Flesh is subject to the Man - yet both flesh and man come under the law in which it operates --

Man of flesh - in flesh - is subject to the law of flesh - he hast the part of flesh - limited it is -- While man is the inheritor of eternal Life - he hast the will - - while flesh is subject to his will - he is the greater

- he (man) is the Greater! - for it is he which has the will - - flesh is nought save the will - for he is as nought without the Will --

= **Survival** =

He hast the will to survive therefore he survives - lest he perish -- I say unto him: "Will to return unto thy Source - thy abiding place"-- The hour hast come when they cry out for surcease from their struggles/ suffering - - yet he wills to survive - knowing not his Source -- He shall be as one which asks of his Source - he shall seek his Source - asking of no man that his survival be assured him -- The foolishness of him which asks of man surety of survival! - for no man can add one hour unto his survival --

= **Science** =

While they think themself wise - learned in the way of science - they know not that they are wanting -- They seek the secrets of "life" in their test tubes - yet they shall not find therein the mystery of Life - for the Father holds within His hand the Secret of Life - for He alone is the Giver - the Bestower - the Knower - the One Which is Perfect - without blame - without shame - - He alone is the UN - the One untouched - without blemish -- So be it they shall seek within the realms of Light - that which is Eternal --

They shall find that they have gone a long way - far afield - looking for the Secrets so carefully hidden up - - while I say unto them: "Come ye up higher - and see ye that which hast been accomplished within the Realms of Light"--

There are things yet to be revealed unto man of science - beyond his highest aspirations - yet he shall be as one prepared to receive - for he as yet is but the babe - he hast but begun his search - - for there are Ones which await his Strength - his maturity - when "he" might be as one responsible for the Greater revelation --

= The Search Shall Continue =

He shall be appraised of his progress - and he shall continue his search - yet he shall search within the Realms of Light - - he shall find therein many new and amazing secrets hitherfore hidden -- Be ye as one responsible for thy part - and ask no man his blessing -- Be ye as one blest to Know from whence thy blessings cometh -- Bow ye unto no puny priest - which sets himself up and praises himself - glorifies himself Be ye as one on whose head I place Mine hand - and ye shall be blest to Know the true from the false -- So be it and Selah --

One to Come

Sori Sori -- Be ye as one blest of Me and by Me - for this have I touched thee - for this have I placed Mine hand upon thee -- Let it suffice that I have blest thee - let it profit thee that thou hast responded unto Mine touch -- So be it ye shall be blest for thy response -- So be it and Selah --

-- I now speak unto thee of One to come -- This One shall come as on wings of Light - - swift in thot shall he come - and by his love and wisdom he is prepared to enter into thy world - and ye shall receive him as One Sent - for I have put Mine Seal upon him - and he shall bless thee by his presence -- Accept him in Mine Name - - so be it that he shall speak for himself - and he shall be given the part which he shall play well -- So be it and Selah --

Out of this World

Sori Sori -- Be ye blest to receive Me - - hold out thy hand and I shall touch thee - by Mine hand shall ye be blest

This is Our time of communication - when we shall enjoy such communication as this -- This is Mine Word unto thee at this time: The way is open for Me to enter into thy world - and it shall be given unto Me to walk with thee as one of flesh - for I shall take upon myself the garment of flesh - and it shall be Mine - and no man shall be unto Me a barrier - for I shall go forth as one fully grown - fully aware of that which is to be done --

I shall not begin My life as an infant babe - born of woman - I shall be as one grown to maturity - I shall do the work of man - and as man of flesh I shall appear - and there shall be no mystery surrounding Mine coming - for I shall come quickly without fanfare -- I shall do that which is given unto Me to do - and I shall depart the way I came - - so be it the Gate swings both ways -- I shall go and come by the same route -- So be it that I shall Know thee - and I shall be reminded of thee -- Ye shall see Me and talk with Me Knowingly --

This is Mine Mission - for it is now come when there shall be closer communion between thee and Me - - I am One of The Host - and I Know the Way - - the way I go - is the way I shall return - for the Gate shall not be closed in Mine face -- Be ye as one prepared to receive Me

- - so be it that I shall make Mineself Known -- This is Mine Word unto thee - - be ye as one alert - and Know ye that I am with thee -- So be it and Selah --

The One to Come

Sori Sori -- The Word I would give unto thee this day - is:- Be ye aware of the One which shall come unto thee - which is the One Sent - for he shall be as one of flesh and bone - - he shall stand tall - and walk as man - look as man - and speak as man - - yet his words shall be Mine - and he shall Know that which he is about -- He shall speak of things familiar unto thee - and he shall be as One prepared to give unto thee a part which shall profit thee --

Let it be for the Good of all - for he shall Know the wisdom of his giving - he shall Know to whom to give and when - - So be it the wisdom of giving -- So be it and Selah --

One to Come

Sori Sori -- Let this be known: That it is now come when there shall be One come into thy midst - which shall be as One Sent - and he shall have a part for thee -- He shall give unto thee a part which shall profit thee - and he shall give thee that which hast been kept for this part - and he shall do his part well - for he Knows his part - and shall be as One prepared to give unto thee that whidh he hast for thee -- So be it and Selah --

Sori Sori -- Have I not said unto thee: "I shall lead thee far afield"? It is but the beginning - and it behooves thee to learn well thy lessons - which shall profit thee -- Ye shall be as one free from all bondage - ye shall have free passage - and ye shall be given free passport into the foreign lands - - far - I say ye shall go far afield - and gather the knowledge which shall profit thee --

Let them profit from thy learning - let them be as ones prepared to learn of thee -- Give not unto them which would rend thee - - let them prepare themself to enter into the Secret places - wherein they might learn that which they have not known --

They speak of the mysteries - yet the mysteries shall be revealed unto them which enter into the place wherein I abide -- I say unto thee: "Come - follow Me - and I shall show thee Greater things than thou hast dreamed of"-- So be it and Selah --

Record for them that which I have shown thee - and they shall put upon it their own interpretation as they are wont to do -- While it is given unto them to know little of that which they interpret - they shall come to know the fullness thereof --

I say: Record that which is possible to pen -- While I know the limitations of pen and paper - the language of man being inadequate - let it suffice that ye use that which is available - and unto them which read:- I say unto thee: read with thine heart - let it be receptive unto Spirit - let it hear that which Spirit sayeth - and ye shall be as one in-Spirited - as one in Spirit - - ye shall be inspired -- So be it ye shall see with the eye of Spirit -- It is said - Spirit is free - it is not limited to - or in flesh - - so be it ye shall be as one free to take thy flight into the places wherein ye know no bounds -- So be it I have spoken - hear ye that which I have said - - let it profit thee to hear -- So be it and Selah - -

As a Honey Bee laden with pollen returning unto her hive - I return unto mine --

In the freedom of Spirit - with my constant companion - I crossed the "RIVER" to a foreign land -- As we stood on higher ground - looking past the Bridge we had just crossed - we saw a grey dreary land - a small train chugged lazily along the bank belching smoke --

We moved on to higher ground - - here we found a "New ground" being prepared for ones yet to come - - the guardian/ agrarian lifts his hand - that we might see in part his project -- Tenderly and lovingly he lifts the cover of the soil (much as a loving nurse would tend a premature baby in an incubator) - a rich golden substance liken unto straw - we observed the soil breating as a mighty lung - fermenting as new wine --

Journeying on we came into the presence of a MIGHTY PHYSICIAN preparing a "TRANSPLANT" on the "GREAT TREE"-- Its roots had been lain bare - exposing its inmost nerves/ vital system - - each root had been carefully lain aside - cut with the utmost precision -- I thot of a heart transplant - my thot was the answered by HIM Who was the SURGEON so skilful:- "Indeed it is a TRANSPLANT --

Entering into another wall-less place - we find a Hostess attending some small children - none over four years of age -- I remembered having been there before - and having partaken of food - - one of the little ones tried to climb on my lap - I reached my hand to assist him - when I realized he was slightly malformed and retarded -- I knew that this child had been aborted by his mother - on the 'other side of the river' -- The hostess asked one - off camera - to bring food -- I said: "None for me "--

Moving on - we come into a place where a foreign language is spoken - - I understood but few words (which I am not permitted to record here) - while I could communicate with the chief inhabitants of the place - - we discussed our travels at some length -- Moving thru the place/ house - I find a man curled up like an embryo - in a fireplace - - great flames leapt before - and over his body --

As I drew nearer for a closer inspection of this sight/ thing - I saw this was a rare find - a strange thing indeed - as a great archeological find would be -- The "man/ thing" had a great treasure - - I saw that it was of rare IVORY - covered with ashes - smoke-stained -- I commanded him to come out - - HE became the treasure - this strange man-like puzzle - so skillfully put together --

As he lay before me - a perfect specimen of HUMAN ANATOMY - I said: "O - what those Doctors would give for this - but I have lost contact with all of them that I used to know - - how could I get this to them? Would it be used rightly? Who would accept it?" The owner had put a price on it that I could not pay - - yet my mind raced on with the idea - the desire to add this to man's store of knowledge - I began at the feet - to disassemble - examine this puzzle - and carefully replace each part - muscles - tendons - nerves - ligaments - bones --

When I reached the chest - opened the rib-cage - I found to my surprise - that it was soft and warm -- I said to one off camera:- Why I could not get this to them over there (the Doctors) - there is life in here - it would take refrigeration - just for this part---

Sori Sori -- Behold Me in this - for have I not shown thee a strangeness? - yet ye shall be given understanding - and it shall increase -- Ask of no man his opinion - and bring unto Me thine gifts - and I shall increase them -- Place thine hand in Mine - and I shall lead thee into greater heights - - Greater shall be thy revelation - Greater thy responsibility - Greater thy reward -- Place thy foot on Higher Ground - and stand ye firm - for I am with thee - - fear not - and be ye as one blest of Me and by Me -- I am He which hast commanded thee: "Come with Me and I shall show thee Great Wonders"-- So be it and Selah --

Sori Sori -- Be ye blest this day - and wait upon Me - the Lord thy God - and I shall deliver thee out of bondage -- So be it and Selah --

Sori Sori -- Mine hand thou hast accepted - - therefore I shall lead thee every step of the way - and ye shall be as one blest -- So be it and Selah --

Sori Sori -- Hast it not been said: Ye shall be delivered out of bondage? So be it and Selah --

Sori Sori -- Put thy hand in Mine and I shall lead thee all the way - - Wait upon Me the Lord thy God - and ye shall be favored -- So be it and Selah --

Sori Sori -- This I would say unto thee this day: It is given unto Me to be One of The Host - and I am come unto thee that ye be as one prepared to enter into the activity which is now under way -- It is with Great joy that I come to thee at this time - for the time is propitious that We come unto thee -- While it is given unto Us to see with Clearer Vision - for We are as Ones on Higher Ground - while thou standeth in the valley - - it shall be given unto thee to see from Our Vantage Point

-- Then ye shall Know that which is meant by the sayings which hast not been fully revealed unto thee --

This is the time of revelation - and it is now come when ye shall stand upon Higher Ground and see that which is being done - and that which hast been done in a short while - - that which ye see is but a fragment of the Whole --

So be it ye see in part only - therefore with limited vision - - this day shall bear fruit -- While ye stand in wonder of the work of man and his attainments - ye shall see Greater things - and ye too shall see the Hand of God Move in Mysterious and Wondrous Ways - which man hast not seen nor reckoned -- This is the time when man shall stand in wonder - and he shall come to Know that there are things yet beyond him/ his knowledge/ his sphere - and he shall reach out for Light - and he shall be given in measure commensurate to his capacity - his effort --

So be it that he shall be given assistance – and he shall find that he hast not found the end -- So be it that he is not alone - Not alone I say! for there is a Mighty Council which is watchful as well as helpful! So be it and Selah -- Let us watch and see that which he does with his knowledge - and let it profit him - let it be for the Good of All mankind - - for progress is progress - and man hast made little progress in the way of Peace --

He speaks of Peace - finds none - yet he hast not done that which leads to Peace -- So be it that Peace comes from within - let it be within him - - therein is the Secret place - wherein he shall find Peace -- So be it and Selah --

Sori Sori -- This is Mine Word unto thee this day: Bless thyself with the Word - bless others by the Word - and be ye as one responsible for thy part -- Let it suffice that I am with thee unto the end - let it suffice them that there is Light - Light sufficient for them which hear - and heed the Word - let them which hear - heed - and be blest --

So be it that there are ones prepared to come into the place wherein I am - and none which are prepared shall be overlooked - for they are accounted for - they are numbered - and sorted - they shall be put into their proper places - and they shall find they have prepared themself for the place wherein they shall be placed -- So be it that each shall be within their proper place - and none shall be out of his proper environment - for this is the day of sifting and sorting - each into his place - for which he hast prepared himself --

Recorded by Sister Thedra

Direction

Sori Sori -- This I would have ye know: I am the Director of this Activity - - the Host of the Host -- This is Mine part: to direct the Host - the Ones which are now prepared to go forth as the Army of Light - as a Great Power - directed by the Lord thy God --

This is the part given unto Me of a Mine Father - under whose command I Am - under Whose Will I Am - - and it is said: "I Am His Will" - it is so - for none have I - - no other direction have I - for I am One with Him - - in Him I live and have Mine Being - none other have I --

So be it that I am the hand and foot of Him - that His Will be done - that He be Honored in Me - and by Me - and thru Me -- So be it and Selah -- Be ye as One with Me - and We shall go far afield - that this be done - that this Work be done unto His Glory -- So be it and Selah - -

Blessed are They

Sori Sori -- Blessed are they which wait upon The Lord - for they shall be served - they shall be given in full measure -- Blessed are they which serve as they are served - for I - the Lord God shall bow before them is servitude -- So be it and Selah --

Blessed are they which go all the way with Me - for they shall Know as I Know - and they shall find Peace - and be forever at Peace - for there is no sorrow within the place wherein I Am -- So be it and Selah --

Blessed are they which Know Peace - for they are the ones which Know the Secret of Peace - they Know from whence they came - the Source of their being -- So be it and Selah --

Blessed are they which Know the Source of their being - for they are One with It - they create like unto their Source - and they are the Anointed of God The Father -- So be it and Selah --

Blessed are the Anointed - for they have received their Sonship/ their inheritance which is given of The Father - they Know their Father as their Source and are One with Him -- So be it and Selah --

Blessed are they which give of themself that others be blest - as they are blest -- So be it that they have received the reward of Services --

Blessed are they which come unto Me - for they shall receive of Me - as I have received -- So be it that I have received Mine inheritance -- So be it and Selah --

Blessed are they which go all the way with Me - for they shall see God - and live forevermore -- So be it and Selah --

Wait upon Me - and ye shall be blest of Him Which hast Sent Me - -So be it and Selah --

Sori Sori -- Let this Word precede the manifestation - for it is so decreed - that One shall come unto thee - and he shall provide thee with the substance necessary for the part which shall be given unto thee -- He shall give unto thee that which hast been kept for thee - and ye shall accept it in the Name or The Father Solen Aum Solen -- So be it it shall be for the Good of All -- So be it and Selah --

Sori Sori -- Blest be this day - for it shall bear fruit - fruit of a New Variety - a Strange New Kind -- While it shall bear new fruit - it shall be as none other - - it shall be sifted - sorted and used for its purpose - - it shall be as fuel for the fire -- So be it and Selah --

Sori Sori -- Bear ye in mind that I am with thee - and fear not - for I am the One Which stands Guard - I stand Porter at the Gate -- I bear thee Good Speed - I give unto thee that which shall profit thee -- So be it and Selah --

Apollo 14

Sori Sori -- It is Mine part to give unto thee this part -- It is given unto Me to see and Know the effort of man -- While he has been as one prepared for this day - this time - this part - - it is given unto Me to have a part in this his effort -- This effort shall be rewarded - this is the time for the reward --

While he hast been alert in his work and effort - he hast but begun his Greater part - - for it is said: Man shall go out in "Space" without his cumbersome gadgets - which is his pride and joy at this time -- These cumbersome gadgets shall be out dated - and man shall find that he is the Greater - - greater than his creations -- So be it that he shall come to Know his potentials --

This is the time for reflection - for the Greater reflection -- I say: Meditate upon the Greater potentials - and be ye as one blest to Know that I am with thee -- So be it and Selah --

"It looks like a plaster mold dusted with grey"

"Its a wild place up here" -Shepherd.

(This is written as Shepherd speaks - alive from Moon) T.

Space Pioneering

Sori Sori -- This is the Word I would give unto thee this day: By Mine own hand they shall be directed - - they shall come into their own - and they shall find that they have been as children playing with toys -- Yet

- I say: Their efforts shall bring great reward - - the effort expended shall be unto them of great value - for - "As ye are prepared so shall ye receive" -- So be it and Selah --

This is no trivial matter - for it is Now Come - when We stand watch - - We See and Know that which is being done - and the purpose for which it is done -- We Know the purpose - We See the efforts put forth -- Now it is Our part to enlighten "them" - to bring forth ones which have the greater knowledge and the Light - the ones which have the Greater part -- These shall be as Sentinels which shall stand ready to assist when "they" are prepared for "The Greater Part" -- While "they" are want to give of themself for the Greater part - "they" are the ones which shall find "their" way - slowly but surely - and this shall profit "them"--

"They" shall be as ones which have earned their passport into the Greater Heights -- So be it and Selah --

"They "- "them" in quotes - refer to us here on Earth - who are in the space race/ age--

Porter Speaks

Sori Sori -- I have given unto thee the Word designed to bring unto thee profit untold - - that which is designed to bring thee wisdom and Light -- So be it that I am with thee that there be Light -- So be it and Selah - -

Shepherd put his foot on the ground (Moon) - his words: "It was a long way - we are here" --

Sori Sori -- Let this be the Word I would give unto thee this day: The beginning of this effort hast begun - and it is for this that We have waited -- We have given unto them the part which hast been given unto Us -- We have placed upon "them" the responsibility which they have accepted -- Now it is said - they shall proceed with the same accuracy which shall lead them into Greater achievements -- So let it be profitable unto all men - all people -- So be it that "they" shall be as the forerunners of the Greater Achievements -- So be it but the beginning --

Sori Sori -- This is Mine Word unto thee this day: Let it suffice thee that I am with thee - and ye shall be as one prepared for a part which shall follow the one just finished - the part which is complete is but the beginning of the one just begun -- So be it that I shall give unto thee the first of this new part on the morrow --

FORECAST

Sori Sori -- By Mine hand shall ye be blest - by Mine hand shall ye be led into the place wherein ye shall find new parts - which shall be brot forth - and which shall be prepared as none before - - for I say unto thee: Greater things are in store for thee than thou hast imaged -- I say: Greater things shall be revealed unto thee - Greater things than thou hast imaged -- Now ye shall be as one prepared - and ye shall place thy foot on Higher Ground - and ye shall stand as a beacon on a hill - and none shall deny thee thy place - for I have prepared it for thee - and none shall cast thee down -- So be it and Selah -- Put thy hand in Mine and I shall lead thee all the way -- So be it and Selah --

Apollo 14 Flight

Sori Sori -- This Mine Word I shall give unto thee - that there be Light in the world of men -- So let it be --

This I would have all men Know: There is a Great and Mighty Host which stands by - that man might be brot out of his bondage - out of darkness -- So be it that We of the Host - have drawn nigh unto them (man of Earth) - and We are in no wise a power of darkness -- We come as a Mighty Power of Light - a Power beyond their knowledge --

We work in concert - as One Man - One Mind - One Purpose - and for this hast man learned the wisdom of preparedness - of Unity -- This is the lesson at hand - which shall be the first of his lessons --

= Unity =

Unity - shall be the Key Word of his success - his Greater accomplishment - - for without Unity - and oneness of purpose - he shall fail in his Mission -- He shall be as the "Loser" - for he shall fail! I say: He shall not succeed in his Mission - he shall fail! --

Now it is given unto Me to Know man's weakness -- I Know his strength - and from whence it cometh -- This is Mine part at this time - to see that he hast the strength to be that for which he went forth - - that he finish that which he came to do -- So be it that he shall be as One prepared for the Greater part --

"Man" hast but begun his Greater Part - his exploration of the Universe - he hast but begun! for the Universe in which he is - is but a small part of the Vastness of so-called "Space" --

= Space =

Space is a relevant word - a word little comprehended by man - for he is so limited in his concept of Space -- He measures space be "rods" - hours - miles - kilometers and the terms familiar unto him - - yet it is inconceivable to him that there are ones within thy midst - from out the Galaxy in which he is - and hast his being --

These have come within thy environment and as guests - and they are not as ones of flesh and bone -- They are real - they are as man with higher intelligence - greater Knowledge - Wisdom - - and they are as the Ones Sent to guide - guard - and direct the worldly - wayward people of Earth - for without Direction the Earth and her inhabitants would long ago have gone into oblivion --

This Great and Mighty Council is as One Great and Mighty Army which stand as ONE - in Unity and Strength - such as man of Earth hast not known -- For this Unity They are powerful - powerful beyond thy present concept --

This I would have thee understand: There is Strength - Power in Unity - and oneness of Purpose --

Therefore it hast been said: "Stand ye with Me - and I shall make of thee a Pillar of Strength -- It is so - - for this have I called forth: "Come unto Me - and I shall lead thee out of bondage" --

This is the day in which man shall find his way - when they which are of a mind to serve with Me - shall find that they are the "Chosen" - chosen for their preparation --

It is said: "As ye are Prepared so shall ye receive" - "As ye are prepared - so ye are chosen"-- So be it there are ones chosen - - these are the ones which have heard - answered - and prepared themself to receive Me- and of Me --

Now hear ye this: There are ones which sit in high places within the world of man - which are prepared for the part given unto then this day. There are ones which sit in high places - which think themself wise - which know not the plan - - while others walk humbly - quietly and serenely amongst them which Know - - and these are the ones which shall be brot out - - these are the ones which walk with surety - they are as ones responsible for their part - for themself - and they are as ones prepared to take their part without the questions and hesitations - known unto man of Earth --

= The Chosen =

"They" walk with head high - confident of their Source - their Strength, their Direction - They are as ones on whose head rests Mine hand in Holy Benediction -- These are Mine Flock" - Mine "Servants" - they serve Me - the Director - - and for this have I classified them as the Chosen - for they are as One with Me by choice - - "They" have chosen to cast their lot with Me -- They cast not lots for the garments - they have cast their lot with Me - that they might find their way back unto their abiding place --

It is said - that: "Their 'passport' is Service" - service unto Life - Light - it is so -- So be it and Selah --

Let it be understood that I am the Wayshower - I lead in the Way they should go - - I direct the way - I Call: "Come ye forth" - and they which hear shall come and receive according unto his preparation --

Let not the hour pass without understanding - - let it be understood that Mine hand is in this - man's effort to arise - to alert himself - to go out from his prison walls - from the gravity of the Earth - the attraction of the Moon -- Yet his efforts hast been as children's play - - yet know ye not that the child at play learns from his toys? - That men learn from his child’s toys? While he hast but begun his greater part - his wisdom is insufficient as yet - - he shall grow in wisdom - and strength as he grows in stature --

He shall grow in stature and he shall become that for which he went forth -- There shall be others come forth to add their part unto that which he hast accumulated in the way of knowledge - Scientific knowledge - - and the Greater part shall become that for which they have worked - - their reward shall be greater than they have imaged --

They shall stand in Awe - in wonder - of the magnitude of the World. The World of Science hast not been "scratched" as We know it.-

It is said: "Come - I shall lead thee far afield" - it is so - - into Greater fields I shall lead thee - so let it be - - for this have I extended Mine hand -- So let it profit thee to accept it in the Name of The Most High Living God -- So be it and Selah --

Search & Research

Sori Sori -- This day shall bring forth the Knowledge of things which have been hidden from thee - - the way of man having been the way of mystery --

The way of man hast led him into this day - and for this shall he find that he hast gone the long way round - for he hast taken the 'long way' - - he hast fortuned for himself the mysteries - the mystery being his unknowing --

The unknowing is the darkness which now weighs heavy upon him. His strength lies within his knowledge of the part he is given - and his will to play it well - unto his own / (light) and profit - which shall profit the Whole --

The Whole is the Unity - the One - and each shall be as the unit of the Whole -- Therefore I say: Take ye note of the effort of this part in which this body functions* -- It is but the beginning of Greater things, Greater knowledge - Greater horizons - for I have said I shall lead thee into far fields -- I have said: "Mine hand is in this" - too - I have said: "Turn from thy ways of war - and seek ye the Light that all men might be lifted up and profit thereby"-- So let it profit thee to be about thy New part -- Seek ye the Light - and be enlightened -- So be it and Selah.

For this am I speaking out -- Let "them" which will revile them which put forth their hand in this effort - be as ones rebuked - let "them" be rebuked I say! - for they know not that Mine hand is in this!

I Say: Mine Hand is in This!

There is Wisdom in Mine Direction - for I Know that which I am about. I Know - I say: "I KNOW THAT WHICH I AM ABOUT!"- Can they say as much for themself? Nay! I say they see not the Plan as I see it. They see as thru a dark glass - with myopic sight - - they clamor for the sake of the puny penny - yet their waste is a pity - their sight short indeed-- "Feed the hungered"- feed them - yea - feed them food which shall nourish them - that which shall keep their body and Soul together and fill their bellies - - then send them into battle - that they might be slain - for Vain Glory? - What profit a man if he lay down his life vainly? How reckons he? How reasons such men?

I say: Feed the hungered - yet let it profit him - - he shall be listed up - and it shall be for the Good of the Whole - for the Good of All that he be lifted up --

*NASA

NOT for Self Sake - but for the GOOD of ALL -- So let it be - - Let it be I say - - let it be for the Good of All -- Amen and Selah --

Count Not the Cost

Sori Sori -- Behold ye the Hand of God Move - See it Move - Know ye that It Moves - - It Moves in ways ye know not - mysterious unto thee which see It --

Know ye that I am come that ye see and Know the Ways of the Lord, that ye have understanding of the Law - the Way of the Law - - and the Way of The Lord shall be plain before thee -- Therefore it is said: "Keep ye the Way of The Lord - and ye shall be led aright"-- So be it and Selah --

Fear nought - walk ye in the Way I lead thee - and no thing shall harm thee - for I am thy Shepherd - thy Strength - thy Shield and thy Buckler --

Blest are they which walk with Me - for they shall not fail - they shall come into the House of The Lord as One with Me - as One of Mine Own - - and these I shall bless - and they shall know no sorrow. So be it I have said: "Come"- and they have come - and these have found their reward - - for their obedience they are rewarded - so be it the Law --

This I would have thee consider: This day is as none other - this is the day of awakening - when they shall come into Greater Light - Greater Heights - Greater Knowledge - - for this have they prepared themself - for this shall they prepare - for it is said: "Prepare thyself-for Greater things than these shall ye do" - it is so -- So be it and Selah --

Now as man prepares the way unto the Greater heights - so shall man follow in his footsteps - for man is his own pioneer -- The pioneers have gone before thee - and thou hast reapt the harvest of their labors. Now it is come when ye shall prepare the way for Generations yet unborn -- Count Not The Cost - - Count not the cost in paltry cents - neither in thy effort -- Yet it is said: "Ye shall not kill" -- When is it said - ye shall call upon thy brethren to give his life that ye might learn of him? I ask of thee: What hast the human sacrifice profited thee? Wherein hast it profited thee? So be it that it is commanded of thee: "Be ye as one prepared for the Greater part" - and no place is it commanded of thee to take thy brother's life! I say - ye shall not kill - - and wherein do I see them crying for blood - trying for supremacy - and wherein do I see them crying out against the ones who reach out for Greater Heights - Greater Knowledge - and Greater Strength --

This I would say unto them which cry out against them which search the skies for Greater Knowledge - the ones which look within the microscope for secrets yet to be revealed - the ones which ask for Knowledge within the Secret places -- These are the pioneers - these are the ones which have prepared themself for the reward which awaits them -- These are as the ones which give of themself that others might know freedom - that others might be blest -- So be it they are the Servants which thou persecuteth -- Hear Me - ye which would raise thy voice against one of these pioneers - for they are the forerunners of Greater things to come -- Be ye not so foolish as to raise thy hand against one of these -- So be it I have spoken - and I shall be heard -- So be it and Selah --

Be ye blest to hear Me - for this have I spoken out this day -- I am He which is Come that ye be blest -- So let it be - - Amen and Selah --

I am Come that All be blest - yet unto them which receive Me I say: Be ye thrice blest - for thou hast received Me and of Me -- So be it and Selah --

I come bearing Good Will unto all men - yet as ye are prepared so shall ye receive - - in the measure ye are prepared so do ye receive - it is the Law -- So be it and Selah --

Mine hand I have placed upon the head of this One which hast received of Me this Word - and I have commanded this be sent forth - that All men might Know that which I have said -- Yet - all men shall not receive it - for not all men have the will to receive Me - neither Mine Word -- So be it that I shall give unto them in like measure - according unto their preparation -- So be it that they which do receive of Me shall Know that they have been blest -- So be it and Selah --

I come as One prepared to lift thee up - for I am Sent at this time - that <u>this day</u> bear fruit as never before -- Therefore I say: "Come follow ye Me - and I shall lead thee out of darkness - out of bondage" -- So be it and Selah --

This is the time of sobering - the time of awakening -- I say: "Look! See! and Know! for the Hand of God Moveth - IT MOVETH!"-- I say: "See ye the HAND OF GOD MOVE - LET IT MOVE!" - and be ye as one moved - for all things shall become NEW unto them which are moved - - for this is the day of Change - and change is GOOD! let it be well with thee --So be it that I have spoken - and I am not finished -- So be it and Selah --

Political - Government

Sori Sori -- By the time they receive this Mine Word - there shall be a change made in the complexion of thy Government - and it shall be for the Good of All - - it shall be provided for - and it shall be according unto the law - that some shall be removed from high places - wherein they sit in power --

Now it behooves Me to say - that Great power shall be given the ones which sit in power - yet that power shall be taken out of the hands of the unjust - for it is the way of some which are given unto some to misuse it --

This I would have thee Know: That I point not Mine finger at the ones which are prone to stand upon the law of: "Justice for All" - these I would separate from the unjust - - and the unjust shall find that they have betrayed themself - for they shall be judged according unto the judgment they have meted out - so be it the law of Justice - "As they have sown - so shall they reap"--

This is Mine Word unto thee: Bear ye witness of Mine Words - and forget not that which I say unto thee - - let it profit thee to remember. So be it that I have spoken - and thou hast heard Me --

The Silent Benefactors

Sori Sori -- Wast it not said that: "Changes shall be made"? - and it is so - - this is well - - so be it it is given unto Me to See and Know -- The changes shall come in rapid succession - and there shall be changes which shall bring about the Greater Knowledge -- While many shall resist the changes - there are Ones which direct them with the Greater Vision - and with Greater understanding --

It is said that ones sit in high places which think themself wise - - and there are Ones which walk within thy midst Silently - unknown - humbly doing their part -- While they are unknown for the most part - they are well known unto Me - - they do that which is given unto them to do - they work silently - without fanfare - and they ask not for reward, they seek no glory - no favors of men - they are as Ones prepared for their part -- So be it they shall do well - that which they came to do -- So be it and Selah --

Progress - Profit

Sori Sori -- Be ye as the hand of Me - and record this Mine Word which I say unto thee - and it shall be given unto them - with that which hast been recorded -- It shall be given unto them as it is given unto thee - - no word shall be changed - for it is given in this manner for a purpose which they know not - - and for thine own sake I say: Be ye as one prepared for the Greater part - let it be - - so shall it profit them to prepare themself for that which is to come --

Wherein is it said:- "There shall be changes"? Let them be as ones prepared for such changes as shall come - for they shall be swift and sure - they shall be as nothing seen before --

These changes shall be Good - I say Good! For they shall be as the part which hast come about by man's own part - that which he hast done. Now it shall be well that it be changed - - it shall be as the poor part which shall give way for the "Greater Part" - - and he shall profit by that which he hast learned from the poorer part -- Let him learn well his lessons - and he shall make way for the Greater lessons which he shall learn from the lesser --

He shall learn well the lessons set before him - fear not! - for he hast but begun the part which is now set before him -- Be ye as one which hast the will to learn - - so let it profit thee to learn well thy lessons -- Learn WELL thy LESSONS I say - for it is given unto man to learn -- Be ye swift to acquire Knowledge which shall profit thee - - so be it that it shall be well with thee -- Amen and Selah --

Sori Sori -- This My Word shall bring unto thee Great Knowledge and Great Joy - for I am come that ye be enlightened - it is for this that I come -- It is now come when ye shall have the part which I have kept for thee - - so let it be as The Father hast Willed it -- Let it profit thee to receive that which I have for thee --

Be ye as one blest to receive that which I have for thee - and ye shall share thy joy with them which have gone all the way with Me -- So be it and Selah --

Sori Sori -- Let the Hand of God Move - let it bring the Light - let it sweep before it the darkness - let it bring the Word into manifestation. Let it be the fulfilling of the Law - - this is the time of fulfilling --

Man shall reap that which he hast sown - the promises shall be fulfilled -- This is the day of maturing - when the Man shall become the Son of God - when the child shall become the man - - and the "Man-child" shall Glorify The Father -- This is Mine Word unto thee - - so let it be understood - this Mine Word - for it shall profit thee -- So be it and Selah --

This is the Time
Initiation

Sori Sori -- This is Mine time - the time in which I shall move amongst men - when I shall touch them - when they shall feel Mine hand upon them - when they shall Know they have been touched --

They shall awaken unto Me - and Know Me as I Know them - when they shall do that which I do --

They shall be as ones receptive unto Me - therefore they shall be as ones awakened - as ones awake --

They shall be as ones prepared to go where I go - do that which I do - therefore they shall be as One with Me --

For they shall be as I am - as the Servant of The Most High Living God - - They shall serve with Me.

They shall dwell with Me - and Know that which I Know - Know as I Know therefore they shall be as ones prepared to do that which I do - go where I go -- So be it and Selah --

Recorded by Sister Thedra

Sori Sori -- Bless the hand which sustains thee - - Blest be the hand which provides thee - - Blest is the one which gives unto thee a hand - the substance which keeps thy hand in motion - which gives unto them the Word -- Blest are they which give of their substance that the "Word" be put forth that others be touched and blest - - blest shall they be - for I shall bless them -- So be it and Selah --

Sori Sori -- Hear ye the Word of the Lord - and Know ye that there is Power in the Word - - and Know ye this: There is Power in the Word which goes out from His mouth - - that which He says is valid - for it is Truth and Light - - it carries with it Great Power and Strength for them which receive it unto themself -- So be it and Selah --

Sori Sori-- For this day let it be said - that the changes which shall come in rapid succession is now begun -- And it shall be fortuned unto some to be the partakers of these changes - which are the forerunners of yet Greater ones -- These changes are but the beginning of yet Greater ones - and none shall stand still -- All shall find that the changes have been part of their life - their being - and environment --

These changes shall bring about other changes which shall benefit the WHOLE -- So be it and Selah --

Fear not the changes - for they are according unto the law of Cause and Effect -- Be ye as one blest - - walk ye with surety - and give unto Me credit for being that which I Am - thy Shield and thy Buckler - - for I shall be unto thee all that The Father would have Me be -- So be it and Selah --

Recorded by Sister Thedra

Mine Servants

Sori Sori -- There are the ones which hear Mine Voice and heed it - - and there are ones which hear it and heed it not -- And unto these I would say: Be ye as the ones which have not heeded - and ye shall wait for a time - - then ye shall know that ye have not given thyself unto Me as Mine Servant - for Mine Servants do that which I give unto them to do - and they are not found complaining - - they are as ones gladly giving and gladly receiving --

So be it that these which have not given unto thee of their substance, of their wealth - their store - that ye be succored - that ye be supplied - shall be cut off for a time --

Then they shall learn that to give is to assist Me in Mine Work - for the Word shall go forth with or without their assistance - yet the ones which assist shall be blest by their own effort - for by their own effort shall they bless themself -- Let them know that they shall be as Mine Servants and they shall do their part - - their part shall be to assist and provide for thee the necessary help - for this part which I have given unto thee --

So be it that I am at the Head of This House - and I have said that Mine Servants shall maintain it in order - and I have set thee over Mine House called the

Gate House

And they which are so blest to receive these words - sent forth - shall be as ones to provide for the maintenance thereof -- So be it that they shall profit thereby -- So be it I shall bless them as they have blest themself - for I shall add Mine Blessing unto theirs - and they shall be thrice blest --

So be it that I have placed upon thy head Mine hand in Holy benediction - and I have given unto thee this part - and it is for this that I have commanded thee that the Word go out unto them which are of a mind to serve Me - of the mind to receive of Me -- So be it - I have spoken - and thou hast heard Me - and obeyed Mine commandment -- So be ye blest of Me and by Me - for I am come that ye be blest --

I Am Sananda

Recorded by Sister Thedra

The Law Shall be Fulfilled

Sori Sori -- Let this be Mine Word unto thee - let it profit them which receive it - - let them accept it in the Name of Him which hast Sent Me. So be it and Selah --

Hold ye fast and fear not - for that which shall come - that which shall be done in the order of which is fashioned by them which shall be caught up in the coming events - - and these events shall be according to the Law set in motion - - each event following in sequence according unto the Law -- So let it be as the Law provides or requires - the Law shall be fulfilled -- So be it and Selah --

This I would say unto thee: The Law is exacting - and no man is exempt from it - for he sets it into motion - and it is fulfilled unto the last farthing -- Therefore it is said: "Obey ye the Law set forth - and ye shall fear not the fulfillment - for it shall be well with thee"-- So be it and Selah -- Put thine hand in Mine - and I shall lead thee into the place wherein there is no fear - no pain - no sorrow -- So be it I am the One Sent that ye be brot out of bondage -- So be it and Selah --

This is the way of righteousness - the way of the Lord thy God - and it behooves thee to hear that which I say unto thee - for it is now come when ye shall be brot up short - for the time draweth nigh when ye shall be as one caught up in the events of the day - wherein there are many strange and wonderful things coming to pass -- Put thine hand in Mine - and ye shall have no cause to fear -- Fret not for them which are caught up in the events of the times - for they are but fulfilling that which is their part --

Put thine own house in order - - let not thy foot slip - prepare thine own self - and wait not for them which have not heeded that which hast been said -- Wait not I say - for them which have not heard - or heeded Mine Word -- This is Mine Word unto thee this day: Pay ye heed - and be ye at PEACE - - hold ye steadfast - falter not wait not - - be ye at Peace I say - - let thy own light shine forth that others see it from afar. Let not the winds of despair flicker thy own light - by their despair and fear - let it burn steadily and forever -- So be it that by thy light I shall find thee -- I say unto thee: Be ye at Peace -- Peace - Peace be unto thee.

Recorded by Sister Thedra

The Early Hours of the New Day

Sori Sori -- The day is but begun - it is yet young - and for this it is the new day - the day is but begun - dawn is now come -- This is the beginning of the "New Age" - wherein the Wonders of the Age shall become common knowledge - unto even the child -- This is the day of Wonders - when they shall stand in Awe of the Wonders which they shall see -- So be it and Selah --

Sori Sori -- Be ye as one responsible for that which I give unto thee to do - and fear not - for I am with thee - that ye be prepared for the Greater part --

Let it profit them to receive of Me the Word - and I shall reveal unto them many things hitherto a mystery -- These which receive of Me shall be blest - they shall find that they have chosen wisely -- So be it and Selah --

= What to Give =

The ones which ask of thee - shall be as ones prepared to receive of thee - the Word -- Let them have that which I have given unto thee <u>for them</u> - - yet they shall be given that which I have given unto thee - as I have given it unto thee - - then they shall do with it as they will - for it is said - it shall be no responsibility of thine - that which they do with it --

They shall bear the responsibility of that which they do with the Word which is given unto them -- They shall be as ones <u>prepared</u> to receive of Me - and then I shall touch them - and they shall be glad for their preparation -- So be it and Selah --

Be ye blest this day - - wait upon Me - the Lord thy God - and ye shall be blest of Me and by Me -- So be it and Selah --

The Touch

Sori Sori -- Let them which <u>will</u> come unto thee - - let them learn of Me - and be as ones prepared for the Greater part - for I shall find them which are prepared - and then I shall touch them - and they shall Know they have been touched -- So be it that I Am Come that they be brot out of bondage -- So be it and Selah --

The Ineffable Word

Sori Sori -- This is Mine Word unto thee this day:- The Word is pure - unadulterated - and for this do I give it unto thee as The Word Ineffable. Bear ye witness of that which I do - that which I say -- Give unto them the Word which is Ineffable - Unadulterated --

Fear not the scorn of man - the way of the dragon - for I say unto thee: The way of the dragon shall be as nought unto thee - for ye shall walk in the Way I set before thee - ye shall fear nought -- Let them which will - speak out in thy favor - - let them which will - revile thee - - and be ye about The Father's Business - so be it it shall profit thee - - So let it be --

One Divided Against Himself

Sori Sori -- For this hour let it be said - that there is none so sad as the one which betrays himself -- It is given unto Me to see them turn aside and become the traitor - - they go part way only - and then they begin the part they create for themself - that which trips them up - - for they forget that which is given unto them thru the Mighty Council-- I say - they begin the web which ultimately entwines them -- Man in his sleep weaves for himself his own web - that which ensnares him -- Now he shall cry: "Let it be cut away"! So shall he learn that he is his own worst enemy - - so let him awaken and arise - come forth from his lethargy - and follow where I lead him - and he shall know no more sorrow--

The Greyness of the Dawn

Sori Sori -- Behold ye the New Day - the day of the Coming-- This is the "Day of The Coming" - this is the "Time of the Coming" - the end of an Age has come - the beginning of a NEW Age -- While the old and the new blendeth as one - it sends off a discordant note - which is of a discordant sound - it is tinted Grey - - grey in nature is it - for it is neither light or dark/ black --

The darkness of the old Age shall be dispelled - as the Son of the New Day ascends the zenith -- The height of the Sun is not yet apparent for man is as yet not prepared to receive the fullness of the Light - he is as one used to the darkness - - the fullness of the Light he could not bear - he is as yet not prepared -- Let him prepare himself - and then he shall look upon the brilliance as one prepared -- So be it and Selah -- For this do I say: Prepare thyself - - for this have I sent forth Mine

Servants that they might come to Know Me - so be it as "they" are prepared -- So be it and Selah --

For this have I spoken out this day - for this have I shown Mineself unto them which have received Me -- So be it and Selah --

On Changes

Sori Sori -- Bless the hand which sustains thee - blest be the hand which provides thee - blest is the one which gives unto thee a hand - the substance which keeps thy hand in motion - which gives unto them The Word -- Blest are they which give of their substance that the "Word" be put forth that others be touched and blest - - blest shall they be - for I shall bless them -- So be it and Selah --

Sori Sori-- Hear ye the Word of The Lord - and Know ye that there is Power in the Word - - and Know ye this: There is Power in the Word which goes out from His mouth - - that which He says is valid - for it is Truth and Light - - it carries with it Great Power and Strength for them which receive it unto themself -- So be it and Selah --

Sori Sori -- For this day let it be said - that the changes which shall come in rapid succession is now begun - and it shall be fortuned unto some to be the partakers of these changes - which are the forerunners of yet greater ones -- These changes are but the beginning of yet greater ones - - and none shall stand still - all shall find that the changes have been part of their life - their being - and environment--

These changes shall bring about other changes which shall benefit the Whole -- So be it and Selah --

Fear not the changes - for they are according unto the law of Cause and Effect - - be ye as one blest - walk ye with surety - and give unto Me credit for being that which I Am - thy Shield and thy Buckler - - for I shall be unto thee All that The Father would have Me be -- So be it and Selah --

The Assistants - Benefactors

Sori Sori -- Be ye as one prepared for to receive Him which is to come. He shall speak with thee as One prepared - as One which hast Mine hand upon him - - for this is He permitted to come unto thee -- So be it that He is from a far and distant land - and He hast the will to speak out that men might have more Light - that there be greater understanding. So be it and Selah --

Be ye blest of My Presence and by Me - for I come that ye be blest. So be it and Selah -- This Mine Word is valid - for it cometh of the Light - with Wisdom - and for the Good of All --

This I would have thee Know: Many await "The Coming" - yet they wait in darkness - knowing not that He is Come -- While He hast as yet not revealed Himself unto All men - many shall see Him and walk with Him - and counsel with Him Knowingly --

This is the time when ye shall bear witness of Me and for Me - for I come as One prepared to see the end of this - Our effort* - and it is given unto Us to Know Our Part - - and none hast the part which belongs unto another -- So be it that I am One of a Mighty Host - and it behooves Me to say unto thee: There are many which make up "The Host" --

There are many which walk within thy midst - which have been Sent -- These are as Ones prepared to serve thee as Selfless Servants of the Light - bearing witness of the Light - and these are as none other -- These are as the Ones alert unto thy needs - they assist in bringing about the necessary supply - the place wherein ye may work unmolested - unhampered -- These bring about certain situations wherein ye might be assisted by them which know not the parts they play in "The Greatest Show on Earth" --

These are as ones walking blindly and obediently - these have responded unto "The Touch"- these know not which hast touched them yet they have responded -- So be it and Selah

For this hast thou been provided -- So be it and Selah --

*Project

They Shall Sleep Their Full Time

Sori Sori -- Let this be Known - that there are ones which walk amongst thee - which are prepared to bring thee out of bondage -- It is now come when they shall make themself known - and they shall be as ones to hear that which is said - and they shall see that which is done --

This is the day of awakening - and they which awaken shall see and know that which hast been done -- They shall go forth as ones awake -

they shall be as ones prepared to awaken others - - yet the others shall be as ones prepared to awake and come forth --

There shall be no abortions in this Mine Work - for they shall be prepared for the awakening - - they shall sleep until they are "Prepared" to awaken --

They shall be as ones which have slept their full time - - then One shall be Sent unto them - and they shall be touched - and they shall respond unto the touch - let it be -- So be it according unto the law - - let it be I say - according unto the law --

Machinery - Past & Future

Sori Sori -- Be ye as the hand of Me made manifest unto them which seek the Light -- Say unto them as I would: They shall heed that which I say unto them - they shall be blest to heed that which I say - for it is now time that they begin to stir - that they be prepared to go out even as I go -- The time swiftly approaches when they shall control the Elements of the Earth - they which are fortuned the Way of the Initiate.

It is given unto Me to Know them which are prepared - them which are trustworthy - - none other shall be admitted into the Secret Place wherein I abide --

This is the beginning of the New Age - wherein the machinery of the past age shall be obsolete - and it no longer shall serve man - as he shall be free from the cumbersome machinery - so heavy and clumsy. For this shall he be as one prepared -- He shall walk without the shoes he needs at this time - for he shall walk touching not the Earth - he shall walk as one without shoes - - for the shoes he shall have no need - for he shall soar as the eagle - as upon wings -- He shall go out as one prepared - for he shall Know the Law which governs this part - - their parts shall be according to the law --

I come that they Know the Law - - the way is clear before them - and it shall be as the Light which guides them --

There are none which shall say thee nay -- I say: Prepare thyself that ye may go where I go - that ye may enter into the Secret Place of The Most High --

Sudden Changes

Sori Sori -- Let it be Known that the time is come when there shall be Great and Sudden Changes - and not one shall escape the effect thereof, yet it shall be for the Good of All mankind --

I say: Forget <u>not</u> that change is Good -- Yet I say unto them: "Be ye as one prepared for the changes"--"Hear ye Me - and be ye as one prepared"--

For this is the day when these things which are prophesied shall come to pass --

Yet I say unto thee: Fear not for I am come that ye be prepared - come unto Me and be ye at peace - - Come I say and be ye at Peace --

Blest are they that come - blest art they which wait upon Me - - let thy hand be Mine hand - let thy feet be Mine feet - and ye shall give of thy time - thyself - thy being - thy All - in Wholly Surrender - - and ye shall have NO fear for I Am thy Shield and thy Buckler --

The Security

Sori Sori -- Mighty is the Word - and powerful it is -- So be it that the Word hast gone forth that there shall be changes - Great changes - - and for this do I say: Be ye as one prepared - and it shall be for thy own good -- It is now come when the Word shall be made manifest - and it behooves Me to say unto thee: Make ye ready for that which shall come for it shall be swift and sure --

None shall escape the changes which shall come - for it is so stated that the time is come when these changes shall be made manifest - and it shall be Good - for it shall be the fulfilling of the law - the fulfilling of the Word -- The Word is valid - and it shall come to pass that one shall stand still while another runs - yet they both shall find themself within the place which they have prepared themself for -- None shall be out of place - neither shall he be overlooked - - he shall be as one numbered and found -- I say unto thee: Fear not - for have I not said unto thee: "I am thy Shield and thy Buckler"? So be it and Selah --

Sori Sori -- For this hour let it be said that the One which shall come unto thee - shall be as One blest to Know that which He is to do - and that which He does shall be according unto the law - it shall be with oneness of purpose - for he is One of the Council - One which hast within His hand His passport - - He shall give unto thee as He hast received -- So be it and Selah --

Sori Sori -- Be ye as the hand of Me and record this Mine Word - which shall be given unto them which are of the mind to receive it -- Let it profit them to receive it unto themself --

This is the Word I would give unto them at this time: -

The day swiftly comes when they shall stand face to face with themself - they shall see themself as they are - - they shall Know themself - and they shall find that they shall be given as they are prepared to receive -- They shall find that their fortune awaits them - - that which they have accumulated shall be their fortune - they shall reap that which they have sown --

They shall be as ones which have sown that which they shall now reap -- The part which they have played - shall be played back unto them - and they shall see that which they have done - and the consequence thereof - - for it is given unto man to read that which he hast written upon the "Book of Life" -- He shall read and Know that which he reads - for he shall be both the Actor and the Audience - the participant in the Great Drama of Life - the Show which is now being played upon the Stage of Life -- I say - it shall profit him/ man - to read and Know that which he reads -- So be it and Selah -- Read and be enlightened - - I say unto him: "Read and be enlightened!" -- For this shall the Book be opened up unto him --

This is Mine Word at this time -- Let them which will - read and learn of Me - for I am The Lord God Which draweth nigh unto thee -- So be it and Selah --

Sori Sori -- Be ye as one blest - for this do I come unto thee - for the time is come that I speak out -- Let it profit them which receive Me, for I come as One Sent of Mine Father--

The way is now open for them which are prepared - that they might enter into the place wherein I Am -- The time of reaping is upon them which have sown unto the Light - for they shall reap the Light - and darkness shall be no part of their harvest -- No sorrow - no shadow shall they know - for they shall walk in the Light - they shall be of the Light.

These shall enter into the place wherein there is only Light - and they shall abide therein -- This is Mine Word unto thee at this hour - - so be it I shall speak unto thee at a later hour --

By the time they have found their way into the place wherein I am. They shall Know the value of The Word - which hast been prepared - - they which have not valued The Word - nor put upon it its value - neither found within it any value - shall not be as ones prepared to enter into the place wherein I Am --

Let it be known that which I have shown thee - and it shall profit them to read that which is recorded - for it is as the Great Play which unfolds before them -- "They" shall come to Know the Value of The Word - to learn the proper interpretation of the Play - of which they are but part --

So let them learn from the Play - from the Actors - that they be better prepared for the Greater part -- So be it the better part of wisdom.

This is Mine Word unto thee at this hour -- Ye shall now add thy part - so be it ye shall be as one blest -- So let it be -- Amen and Selah

The Play

There is a Great place within the Gate - - I shall liken it unto a glorified "Disney Land" -- Instead of calling it "Disney Land" I shall refer to it as Sananda - Wonder - Land --

Round about it on the outside - the ground is covered with 3 inches of glorious white snow --

There are places for the travelers to stay - small private houses - like way stations along the way --

The snow around some - is still fresh and sweet - pure and white -- Everywhere there are many intertwining tracks - like unto cycle tracks - one crossing another - in an endless crisscrossing pattern --

My Companion - Elder Brother (Tall & strong) - had been within the Gate - seen the Wonders therein - had now come out to assist the nearest ones - who had set up camp in one of the small houses -- As we moved over the snow - I said to the Brother: I have found if I hop (as if both feet tied together) like this - its easier than trying to make my way in all that maze of tracks - they are a hazard --

We slimmed over them - as a butterfly over a flower bed --

He went a farther distance to his place - while I stopped at mine for a moment - - he returned for me -- We then went to the house where the snow had been trampled down - becoming slush and soil -- Here I found my "Mama and sisters"-- I saw they were busy with "puny activity" "much ado about nothing" --

When I ask if they were ready to go into this beautiful place of activity - Mama said: I don't believe they will want to go today - they have gone - (on some activity of their own) - (this activity was unfamiliar to me) --

This was inconceivable unto me - for to come so close and not go in was unthinkable to/ for me -- It would be like unto a child being a block from Disney Land - and not being allowed to see the Wonders therein --

I wept with sorrow - for their ignorance -- I say: They Know Not that which they deny themself - or now refuse - - they haven't learned the Value of travel -- They have no idea of the Wonders within that Place -- I likened it unto a Great Fair --

= Blessing =

Sori Sori -- Hail Hail unto thee - Hail unto thee O Mighty Son of God. Born of <u>woman</u> art thou - yet I say unto thee: Hail Hail O Son of God. Mighty - O Mighty art thou -- Thy presence is required within the Earth for it is the time when ye shall do that for which thou didst come -- So be it and Selah -- Blest art thou - O Son of God - born of woman -- Let this be the Word I would give unto thee this hour --

To Become a Son of God...

Sori Sori -- Let this be Mine Word unto thee this day - and ye shall be blest to receive it -- So be it and Selah -- To become a Son of God by adoption - one hast to be as The Father would have them be - they shall be as one prepared to enter into the place wherein He is -- They shall give of themself that The Father be Glorified -- They shall honor The Father by their presence - by their being as He would have them be - pure of heart - even as He is pure --

This hast been one of the Secrets which man hast not understood: The "Pure of heart" "Pure even as He is pure"-- The pure of heart is one which hast turned from his willful way - and surrendered his will unto The Father's Will - to serve Him as His hand and foot made manifest - that He be Glorified on the Earth and in the Heavens --

There is none other which can be considered pure of heart - for they are willful of heart - they seek the things which are of the world - they seek glory for self -- They ask that they be brot out of bondage - that they might be free - - say nothing of the brother left to be devoured by the darkness --

I say: To serve the Light selflessly - is to be as The Father would have thee be -- So be it and Selah --

Alert!!

Sori Sori -- This is Mine time with thee - and it is the part which I have kept for thee - that I shall now give unto thee -- This is the part which hast been kept for this day -- The time in now - when We shall be as One prepared for that which is to do - - the time is Now Come when We shall do that which is given unto Us to do --

There shall be a place provided for each and every one which goes forth out of the physical body - - each one shall find that he is prepared for the place wherein he is received --

There shall be room aplenty and to spare - - there shall be no rush - no over crowding -- The way is prepared - each shall be received into his proper place - according to his preparation - so be it the law - and the Plan which is unfolding before thee --

There is not one which shall be out of place - each shall be within his own place - according unto his own preparation -- There shall be a Great and Mighty onrush of Assistants - which stand ready to assist -- There shall be the Ones which have gone before - which have made such progress that they are now prepared to go forth to receive them which are yet to come - the ones which are to come --

This is the way of the Lord - that each be prepared for his part - his place - - as he is prepared so shall he receive - - as he receives so does he give - he gives in like measure unto his receiving - for as he is prepared - so does he go forth to serve his fellow men --

This is selfless Service - for they which serve the Light Know the value of Service - Know the joy of Serving as they have been served. So be it that they serve as One - with Oneness of Purpose - - that each might go forth - that his fellows be lifted up -- So be it and Selah --

Say unto them: There shall be a great gathering in - a great coming in - and it behooves Me to say unto them: "Lift up thine eyes - from whence cometh thine help"-- Ask of the Light that ye be prepared for the Greater Part - so let it profit thee - - so shall it be for the Good of All -- So may it be - as The Father hast Willed it --

I say unto thee: Heed that which I say unto thee - heed ye THAT WHICH I HAVE SAID UNTO THEE - and be ye as One Alert - for the time is NOW COME that ye shall SEE THE HAND OF GOD

MOVE -- The tide shall be staid - the air shall be rent - the air shall be as polluted - the flesh shall be torn - the hands shall be bloody - the head shall be as torn away - the parts shall be separated one from the other - and not one shall be left for the vulture -- So be it that I have said: Fire and water shall mix - and it is so – The mountains shall bow low - the rivers shall raise up - - yet man shall be as ones prepared for his NEW Place - for it is said: "Man" is Eternal - - man is man - and he comes under the law--

Now it is said: AS YE ARE PREPARED SO SHALL YE RECEIVE --

Be ye as one prepared to follow where I lead thee - that ye might go where I go -- So be it ye shall have no fear - for I Am The Lord thy God Sent that ye be lifted up -- So be it and Selah --

I Am He Which is Come that ye be lifted up - therefore I say: "Come - seek ye the Light and ye shall NOT taste of 'death' "--

Let this be Mine Word unto them which are of the mind to hear and heed -- So be it that this Mine Word shall go forth that they might Know what I have said -- So be it I have sent it forth - it is valid - and the Word shall stand as a testimony of the Word Immaculate - - the Word shall not become invalid - by man nor time -- For this do I say: "Prepare thyself for the Greater part" - - it is the Law that ye be prepared - that ye be warned - - therefore I say: Heed that which I say unto thee - that ye be prepared - for it is thine own responsibility to prepare thyself -- So be it and Selah --

Recorded by Sister Thedra

One in Jeopardy

Sori Sori -- Beloved: It is the time of change - and change shall bear witness of the times - for it is now come when the changes shall be swift and sure -- So be it that it shall hold true for the way of man - for man shall change his ways - - and he shall be as the one which hast placed himself in jeopardy - he shall be as one which stands upon the ground which he hast fortuned himself -- He shall be as one which hast made his own bed - and he shall find it hard -- So be it that he shall arise and run from it - he shall be as one which runs and looks not back for he shall see the folly of his way - and return not again -- So be it and Selah --

One to Come

Be ye as one prepared to receive the One which comes in Great Glory and Love - for He comes even as I - - He hast the part which is given unto Him of The Mighty Council - for He hast proven himself prepared for the part which He is to play in this - the Greatest Show upon Earth. So be it it shall profit thee to receive Him and of Him -- So be it and Selah --

Be ye as one blest of Me and by Me - for I speak unto thee as One of the Host - as One approved by The Mighty Council --

I come in Love - and with Authority - for I am given the privilege of speaking as One of The Host - as One of "The Greatest Show on Earth" --

There are many Actors - many I say -- Many there be - each hast his own part - yet each part is part of the Whole -- for All parts are put together to make up the Whole --

There are no "small" parts - no parts which are unnecessary unto the Whole --

This is the day when We shall stand revealed before man as the Great and Powerful part of the - wherein there is no discord - no dissension - no disharmony - no dissatisfaction --

There is Joy in serving the / - and being the Assistants of Our Bright and Shining One - the One which hast given of Himself that We be lifted up - prepared for the Greater part -- The One which hast proven Himself - that "He hast so loved the world that He gave His life for them"--

This One - the Bright and Shining One - is The Lord God - which hast prepared the Way for Us - for thee - for them which have the will to enter into the place wherein there is no darkness -- So be it that I am come even as He - - I come that there be Light / -- I walk with sure foot, I walk with surety - oneness of purpose - there is no doubt within Me - I sleep not - for sleep is no part of Me - I Am Awake!

I am watchful - I speak unto thee in the hours of thy sleep - and thou hearest that which I say - - some thou hast remembered - some ye shall recall - some ye shall put within thy closet until the need for such store. Yet it is not forbidden thee to enter into thy closet that ye be enlightened.- So let it profit thee that which is stored within the store-room of thy being --

I say: Thou hast a rich store - - partake of it as it is necessary - draw upon the fullness thereof - and it shall be replenished - for it shall be replenished and filled unto overflowing -- Let it be - for I have a Great amount of store for thee - - I say - partake of Mine store - and I shall be glad -- So be it and Selah --

Give unto Me credit for being that which I Am - and I shall come unto thee as One of thy Benefactors - prepared to receive thee unto Mineself as One with Me - and We shall be of One mind - One purpose, One plan - - and in Him We shall abide as His hand and His foot made manifest -- So be it and Selah --

The harvest is ripe - and the laborers are now prepared to go forth to gather in the harvest -- Let it profit thee to go forth as one of the reapers - for thou hast sown goodly seed and well - thou hast attended thy field - now ye shall find thy harvest good -- So let it be the Will of The Father that ye be brot in as one filled - and fulfilled -- So be it and Selah --

Our Visions

Sori Sori -- Bear ye in mind I am thy Lord and thy God - both the hearer and the asker - I am the hand and the foot of The Father made manifest unto thee -- I pay homage unto thee - and I seek thee out in the hours of thy sleep - - I speak unto thee in the hours of sleep - I make for thee lessons yet to be read and learned - - as for thy learning - it is not complete -- I say unto thee: Ye shall learn that which I have prepared for thee - and it shall be well with thee -- So be it and Selah --

The Joy of Serving

Sori Sori -- It is with Great Joy that I come as One prepared to assist thee in thy part which thou hast chosen -- It is for this that I have spoken unto thee of things to come - of the changes which are to be -- The time is at hand when the changes shall be as one - for one shall lead unto the other - - for that do we see it as the "Day of change" - "The time of change -- The changes shall be as part of the day of change --

The day of rapid change is come - when these things shall be as part of the "end time" - and the end time is now upon thee --

For this do We say: "Come ye forth and be ye as <u>one</u> prepared for the New Day" - for thy new part - - for Greater Glories await thee -- Pay ye heed - and waste not thy time in mournful sonnets of by-gone times - - bygone let them be - let them pass as the night -- Look unto the Morn - look unto the Sunrise of the New Day -- Mourn not for the dead - rejoice for the risen / -- Let it be said: "The Lord is Come - rejoice ye - it is so - - Praise The Father Solen Aum Solen - Praise ye His Holy Name - give unto Him All the Praise and the Glory - for He is The Giver of All Good things - He is The Cause of thy Being -- So be it and Selah --

The Sure Foundation

Sori Sori -- Upon this Foundation I have builded this Mine Temple - and upon this Foundation I shall build yet Greater -- Greater Work shall I do - for it is but the beginning of the New Day in which I shall do the Greater Work - the Greater things -- These are the things of which I speak - and none shall rise up against Me - for I shall set up a bastillian/ a fortress against Mine enemies - wherein they shall not enter -- So be it that they which set themself against Mine Servants shall find that they have betrayed themself - that they have been their own worst enemy - for they shall find that they have set their own trap - wherein they have entrapt themself --

This is the time in which to consider well the Word which I speak in which I say: "Prepare thyself for the Greater part" - - put forth thine hand and I shall lead thee far afield - and I shall not forsake thee -- Be ye as one blest to receive Me and of Me - - be ye mindful of Mine Servants and bless them as I have blest thee -- For this do I say: Be ye as One - One with Me - and ye shall Know as I know -- So be it and Selah --

So be it I am come that All be blest - - yet they which come shall be received of Me and by Me -- So be it and Selah--

Seek Ye the Light

Sori Sori -- For this hour let it be said - that I have gone the long way round - to give unto thee this Word -- It is for this that I have called thee from thy bed -- Ye shall be as one responsible for this Word which I give unto thee for them - - they shall find it profitable to receive it - and it shall be as the warning - and as the Word of The Most High God. They shall be as ones alerted! and therein is Wisdom --

There shall be few which shall heed this Mine Word - and these I shall bless -- The ones which reject Mine Word shall find that they are like unto ones which have thrown overboard their own life-belt - they shall be as ones which hast betrayed themself -- It is now come when I say: Turn ye unto the Light - Seek ye the Light - Know ye the Light - for it is now come when ye shall cry for assistance -- I say I am come that ye Know no sorrow - that ye be delivered out of bondage -- So be it that I stand by - ready to assist thee - yet ye shall first accept Me for that which I Am - ye shall be blest to accept Me -- So be it and Selah.

By the time ye receive this - it shall be that One hast gone forth as a Swift Messenger - unto the ones which are prepared -- This One - the Swift Messenger shall be as One on whose shoulders is placed the responsibility of alerting them which are prepared to. These shall heed - these shall be glad they have heard and obeyed -- So be it and Selah - -

By Mine own hand have I given unto thee the Word which hast been spoken by Mine Own Mouth - - for from Mine own Mouth hast the Word gone forth - and by Mine own Power have I recorded this Mine Word which I have spoken -- I have been as One on whose head Mine Own Father hast lain His Hand - - therefore I have touched Mine own and she hast in turn received Me - and as she hast received Me - therefore ye shall receive of her this Mine Word - - so let it profit thee.

This I would say unto thee Mine Own: Give unto them the Word - let it go forth - and let them do with it that which they will - - for this is thy part - they shall do with it that which they will - that is their responsibility! --

The hour strikes when they shall choose which way they shall go. The Way is set before them - they shall choose their way - they shall be as one responsible for their choice!

Ye shall not fear for them - neither shall ye grieve for them which betray themself - for it is not Mine purpose to place their responsibility upon thine shoulders - - let them take their own responsibility - and be as ones prepared --

The time is at hand when I say:- Put aside thy own preconceived ideas of Me and about Me - for I come in Spirit - - I come crying unto thee: "Look up - See the Dawn of the New Day - - See the Glorious New Dawn - - Wait not for another - this is the New Day! THIS IS THE NEW DAY - - I say - WAIT YE NOT FOR ANOTHER!" --

Wait not for the Coming of One which hast Come - while thou hast slept! --

I say unto thee: There are ones which hast borne witness of Me - they have Seen Me - and Counseled with Me - - they have spoken of Me - borne testimony of Me - yet they are without honor amongst them which believe Me not - - they are ridiculed and reviled for thy sake --

I say:- Ye shall find that I forsake not Mine Own - I shall NOT forsake nor turn away from Mine Own -- I too say - that Mine Own Know Mine Voice and answer Me - they respond unto Mine touch - they bear witness of Me -- So be it that I Am Come - even as I went - I Come!

Arise - Alert thineself - and be ye as one awake! for I shall shew thee the things which ye shall do - - I shall be unto thee sufficient unto thy need -- Break bread with Me and I shall supply thy needs -- I shall shelter thee with Mine hand - and I shall direct thy way - and be thy refuge in the time of storm -- So be it and Selah -- I am The Lord thy

God - - be ye as one prepared to receive Me and of Me -- So let it be profitable unto thee --

This day is the one foretold - wherein many shall go forth to bear testimony of the Word - and to bear witness of the Word which goes out from Mine own Mouth --

Let thy Voice be raised in Praise - sing ye a glad Song - walk ye with surety -- Know ye that I Am Come - that I Am with thee - - bear ye witness of Me - let thy Light so shine that they might see it from afar.

Bring unto Me thy Gifts - put them in Mine hands that they be Mine that they be used for the upliftment of man -- Put thine hand in Mine that I might direct thee - - hear ye that which I say unto thee - and fear not - for I Am Come that ye be lifted up -- So be it and Selah --

(He knocked on the door three times - then He touched me - arousing me from a deep - deep sleep - to take this dictation) T.

Sori Sori -- Be ye as one prepared for that which ye shall do - for I shall give unto thee a part which shall be different and new unto thee. So be it that ye shall go into a place wherein there are ones which await thy coming - and they shall be as ones prepared to receive thee -- So be it and Selah --

Sori Sori -- Hold out thy hand and I shall take it - I shall lead thee every step of the way -- Know ye not that I am with thee unto the end?

Hast it not been said that I shall direct thee - and I shall not fail thee?

Be ye as one blest of Me and by Me -- Keep thine hand in Mine - and ye shall not fail - - Let thine hand be Mine --

Let thine time be Mine - and We shall be as One -- Let it be Known that which I say unto thee --

Praise ye the Name of Solen Aum Solen - for He is the Source of Our Being -- So be it and Selah --

They Shall Obey Mine Voice

Sori Sori -- This day is the day for which they have waited - the Day of Salvation - the Day of "The Coming" - the Day of Deliverance -- I say: "Wait no longer - for the Coming - for I AM COME" -- I Am Come with the Host - Mighty and Strong - prepared to go forth as Mine Ministering Assistants - as Mine Hand made manifest unto them which slumber --

Now they shall stir - and be as ones quickened - - then I shall touch them and speak with them - counsel them - lead them in the way they should go -- These shall hear Mine Voice and obey it - they shall arise at Mine touch and do Mine bidding - - they shall Know the true from the false - for the false shall mimic Me - that he deceive them which have not been touched --

They shall be as ones deceived and they shall follow the deceiver - declaring falsely that they have known Me as their Savior - as their Master - as their Servant -- Yet know ye this:- I am not the deceiver - I make no promises that I am not prepared to fulfill -- I say unto thee: Try Me - give unto Me credit for being that which I Am - and I shall do

Mine part -- Look not for signs and miracles - for I make no show to satisfy thy curiosity -- I say unto thee: Try Me - obey ye the law - walk ye as one sober - give unto Me thy hand - and I shall lead thee in paths of righteousness - - I shall counsel thee -- Ask of Me and be ye as one blest - heed that which I say --

Do thy part and I shall do Mine - - rest thine head on Mine bosom - and ye shall find peace therein --

Let Peace be within thee - let thine hand be Mine - and ye shall do that which I do - - ye shall walk with Me - go with Me where I go - Know that which I Know - rejoice with Me -- So be it and Selah --

Ye shall have no need for soothsayers - no need for charlatans - no need for the gadgets which are designed to enlighten or emancipate thee for I have said I shall touch thee - and ye shall Know - - ye shall be blest as I have been blest --

While it is said: "Ye shall Know as I Know" - let it be understood that ye grow in wisdom - - ye shall grow to maturity -- The child grows/ the man-child shall grow to maturity - unto the strength wherein he shall bear the responsibility of the Adulthood - the Manhood - the Adeptship - the Initiate -- He shall be as one prepared to walk with Me, go with Me where I go -- So be it that I have said: "Come unto Me and I shall give unto thee as thou art prepared to receive" -- So be it and Selah --

This I would have thee Know:- PROVIDE THINESELF WITH THE PROPER CREDENTIALS - and I shall give unto thee passport into Mine place of abode - wherein ye shall abide with Me - rejoice with Me - - and wherein no harm shall come unto thee -- So let it be as ye have prepared thyself -- So be it and Selah --

The Two Paths

Sori Sori -- Let this be Mine Word unto thee this day -- Let it profit "them" to accept it in Mine Name - for they shall come to Know the true from the false - they shall find that the enemy is the enemy - that he is the deceiver - - he lies in wait to ensnare them - he is merciless and filled with deceit - he is cunning -- He is not of a mind to let them go - he finds means in which he can hold them bound -- He hast the blood of generations upon his hands - the blood of the innocent - the unborn -- He whispers the promises of his deceitful plan - he finds ways in which to distract them - he gives unto them that which flatters them, they accept it because of their own ego - their desires -- "They" have not yet learned the way of the wise - the way of the Initiate --

They seek the way in which they go - for the glitter - flattery - ease and the praise of others - - they have not found Mine Way attractive - for it is said: "It is not the popular way - it is not the easy way" -- Wherein have I said they shall choose - they shall be as the one to choose which way they go? None bring them against their will - - so let it profit them to choose wisely the path I have pointed unto them - let them walk therein and be blest --

Let them find their way - let them wait -- Be ye not downcast - for they are as the green nut - they shall find - their time cometh swiftly - when the winds shall shake the tree - and the ripe nuts shall fall into the harvest - be gathered in - - the green ones shall be left -- So be it and Selah --

Thy Wayshower

Sori Sori -- On Mine High Holy Mount I stand - - I see that which goes on within the valleys - within the shadows --

I am not of the Earth - I am of the Light - I stand within the Light - I am not limited unto one place - one time - one hour - - I am not of a season - - I am One with Mine Father - I am Eternally His Son - none can deny Me Mine inheritance --

This I say unto thee: Be ye not moved by their arguments - let them argue among themselves - and be ye no part of their foolishness - for I am thy Wayshower and thy Shield and Buckler -- Be ye not persuaded by their arguments - for they but I have their own puny opinions and ideas on which to base their arguments --

Let the Light shine forth - let them which will - see and be blest -- So be it that I shall lead him which wills to come unto Me -- This I say unto All: "Come - Come and I shall lead thee safely"-- So be it and Selah --

The Light Shall Sustain Thee

Sori Sori -- Be ye blest this day - let thy hand be Mine - and give unto them this Mine Word --

There are many which have denied the Word - which turn away from Me - - yet I say unto them: "Come - Come unto Me and I shall lead thee"-- It shall profit them to hear Me - and to answer - to come - and they shall not want - for I shall sustain them - - I shall be their Shield and their Buckler --

Wait not for Signs and Miracles - - listen ye for Mine Voice - - Know ye that I Am with thee - and I shall protect thee in the time of stress -- Turn unto the Light - Seek the Light and fear not - for the Light shall sustain thee in the hour of trial -- Faint not - weary not of Mine Sayings - for they are given unto thee for thy own sake --

I neither fail - nor discard that which I give unto thee - for Mine Sayings are valid - according unto the law -- It shall profit thee to accept them for thy own - and ye shall abide by the law --

Therefore I have given unto thee the Whole of the Law - - now it behooves thee to abide by it -- Wall ye with surety - - cast out thy puny opinions/ preconceived ideas of Me/ about Me - and listen - that I might speak unto thee THIS DAY --

Bear ye witness of Me and Mine Word -- Let thine feet be Mine - walk ye in the Way I go -- Sing ye Praise unto the - let thy heart sing - let thine Song be a Song of Praise unto thy Source - Solen Aum Solen for He is thy Source --

Let not thy FOOT SLIP - let thy feet be shod with the Light -- The wings of the Dawn shall be upon the feet of them which walk with Me for they shall be as ones with wings upon their feet - they shall run and not tire - they shall go and come as I go and come - and time shall be as nought -- Distance shall be as nought - for they shall be prepared to go where I go -- This is Mine Word - which shall be valid unto All which apply the law - comply unto it -- These shall be as ones prepared to go with Me into the Secret places wherein there is no darkness - no bondage -- So be it I have spoken --

Mine Servant hast heard - and recorded it for thee - - now ye shall remember the Servant as Mine hand made manifest unto thee - and be ye blest to remember -- So be it and Selah --

What of him?
The Sower

Sori Sori -- The day is now come when it is expedient to say unto thee: The part which is given unto thee is for thy own sake - and ye shall be as one responsible for thy own part - each for his own -- While there are ones which look unto another part with envy - or point his finger at another and say: What of him? -

I say unto them: Be ye about thine own part - and let "them" be - for they are of no concern unto thee - - each shall do his part - and prepare himself for the GREATER PART -- Let it be said that one shall sow - another shall follow him and reap -- Therefore I say unto thee: Sow ye that which ye would reap - sow ye not pricks for thine brother's feet --

Sow ye seed which shall profit him - and ye shall reap accordingly. As ye have sown so shall ye reap -- Prepare the field for the one which shall come after thee - that he might sow the seed for the harvest yet to come --

This is the Word I would give unto them which have gone forth to sow: The day of reaping shall come - let it be a bountiful harvest - profitable unto thee -- So may it be --

Be ye as one blest --

The Traitor

Sori Sori -- Lo it is Come when there shall be one which stands in high places - which will betray himself - for he shall give unto himself the credit and the glory which is not his -- He shall be as the two tongued serpent - which hisses and his tongue shall spew venom --

Look - See and be aware of his work - - yet ye shall not be as one deceived by him/ that which he says - for he shall be as one with two tongues - he shall speak words of honey - which shall drip from his lips as honey from the comb - - with the other tongue he shall spew venom which shall poison the honey --

Let it be Known - that which I say unto thee - for he shall stand tall in the places of high esteem - yet he shall contaminate the spot wherein he stands - for I say he is not that which he would have them believe - - Let it be said that there are some amongst them which would lift them up - they shall bear with this one - yet he shall be a thorn in their flesh --

I shall not put Mine finger on him - I shall not point him out - - yet ye shall know him for that which he is -- Be ye as one watchful - be no part of his work - for it is not of Me - - he hast been Mine foe -- While I say he is Mine foe - I turn not from him - I await his time - for <u>his</u>

time shall swiftly come -- As the seasons - so shall his time come - - be ye not one to set foot against him - - yet I say - be ye no part of his work, his foolishness --

So be it I have spoken and thou hast heard Me -- Let it suffice that I am with thee - - so shall it be --

Each to His Own Place

Sori Sori -- Be ye as one prepared for the part which I shall give unto thee for them which await it -- Be ye as one on whose shoulders rests the responsibility of this part -- Give it unto them as I give it unto thee. So be it ye shall be as one blest --

There shall be a place prepared to receive each and every one which comes into the place wherein they shall be received -- They shall be received within the place wherein they are sorted - numbered - and placed within their own place - their own environment --

They shall be as ones gathered - as ones which have found their own kind - their own people -- They shall be blest according unto their preparation - as they are prepared so shall they receive --

Now it is said - and rightfully so - that: "There are none so sad as the one which betrays himself"-- This is the pity of the one which cries out for help - for he hast been given the Word - and he hast not accepted it - he hast gone his own way - heeding not that which was designed for hie own Good - for his own welfare --

I say: Behold him in his pity! Behold him within his own place - where he cries out for help -- See him as he is - know ye that he cries for mercy - - yet mercy is shown him - for he shall learn wherein his freedom lies - and he shall turn unto the Light -- In full Light he shall Know that which he hast done - and wherein he hast failed --

So be it that he shall be strong in his deliverance - and he shall stand as a living witness of the Mercy and Love shown unto him - for he shall be as one delivered out in time of his restitution -- So be it and Selah - -

Now ye shall consider well the part of the Servant which hast served well the Light - for he shall be one with it - and he shall be as one prepared to enter into the place prepared for him - wherein there is no darkness - no cry for mercy - for he shall Know no sorrow - no pain - no sadness shall be his lot --

So be it that he shall walk the planes of Light - wherein there are no pitfalls - he shall know wherein he walks -- He shall abide within the Light and be as one "Enlightened" -- So be it and Selah --

I say he shall be unbound - he shall be as one free from all bondage - he shall be free from the gravitation of the Earth - and free from the attraction of the Moon -- So be it and Selah --

Sori Sori -- By Mine hand shall I lead thee - and by the Word shall ye be prepared -- So be it and Selah -- Be ye as one prepared - and Know ye that I am with you -- Be ye blest this day -- So be it and Selah.

Dedications - Oneness of Purpose

Sori Sori -- This is Mine Word unto thee this day:- Bear ye witness of Me - and give unto them this Mine Word - - let it profit them to receive it - for it shall profit them --

There is none other which is the Lord God of Earth - none other Sent to do that which is given unto Me to do - - for it is given unto Me to See and to Know that which goes on within the Realm of Light - for I Am of the Light - I work within the Light - and with the Light -- I Work as The Father Wills - for I Am the WILL of The Father made manifest - as One brot forth that His Will be done -- I Am the "ONE SENT" that ye of Earth might Know His Will - that ye might Know as I Know --

HE IS THE SOURCE - I am but the Son of Him which hast begotten Me -- So be it that I Know Mine Father - The Cause of Mine Being - - therefore I say unto thee: "Come and Know ye as I Know" - follow where I lead thee - and all shall be well with thee -- Bless thyself as I have blest thee - for I have given of Mineself that ye might come to Know as I Know -- So be it that I give unto thee as ye are prepared to receive -- So be it and Selah --

Call unto Me and I shall bear thee -- See ye that which I do - and take ye heed of Mine Work - and do that which I give unto thee to do. Resist not the changes which come about - for there shall be changes aplenty - and to spare!!!

Fret not for the times - the appearances of the day - for they can deceive thee - they can confuse thee -- Hear ye Me - and be ye as one prepared for that which I give unto thee to do - for it shall be as nothing else thou hast done -- So be it that I am with thee unto the end -- So be it and Selah --

Forget not that which I have said: "There are none so foolish as the one which thinks himself wise"-- So be it and Selah --

For this have I spoken - that you be blest as I have been blest --

Recorded by Sister Thedra

THE SCHOOL OF MELCHEZEDEK

= The Word =

Sori Sori -- Hast it not been said that thy work is not finished? Hast it not been said that greater shall ye do? So shall the Word be fulfilled So be it and Selah -- Sealed is THE WORD ---

= Truth =

Behold ye in me - the Word - for I am the Word - - I am he which is sent that ye have The Word -- I am he which IS come that ye might KNOW -- So let it be as the Father hast willed

Behold ye in me the Truth - the Way - the Life - the Light which I Am I come that ye might be brot into the realm of Light wherein there is no darkness - no sorrow - no uncertainty ---

= The Traveler =

For the way unto mine place of abode is Light -- While the adepts keep the way - the children of the Father walk within the way - and falter not when the climb is steep - the valleys dark and oppressing --

They press on - knowing they are not alone - that there is One Who beckons them on - who calls unto them saying: "Fear Not - Fear Not - FEAR NOT - for I am with thee unto the end"

= **The Call** =

Arise mine children unto the way which I lead thee -- Arise! Arise! Come forth! and ye shall find that thy travels - thy travails have not been in vain - for they are as nought unto thy joys - when thy foot hast been set upon the heights -- And then thou canst see wherein thou hast labored and won the victory -- Then ye shall turn with joy to give a hand unto the one which follows after thee - and ye shall be as an "Elder Brother" unto him - even as I am unto thee --

I say: "Fear Not!" for I have gone before thee that ye might find thy way -- And be ye not deceived - - I too - have walked the same path that ye now tread - -

I too - have prepared mineself for the victory won - -

I too - have walked the valleys and the steeps - - the crags I have scaled - the rocks have bruised mine body - the darts have pierced deep within mine body - - and yet - I won the victory over flesh -- The spirit prevailed over death - and I now stand upon the High Holy Mount as one prepared to assist thee in thy flight ---

= **The Master** =

I say - I am prepared to assist them in thy flight -- And ye too - shall be as the Victor - and ye too shall praise the name of Solen Aum Solen as I -- Ye too - shall know Him as I know Him - - and be ye as one prepared even as I - - for this I say unto thee in His Name - that His Will be done So let it be ---

(Come ye at another hour - and be ye blest for thy coming)

= Loyalty =

This is mine word unto thee - and it behooves about the Father's business - even as I -- And at no time shall ye betray thyself - at no time shall ye turn from thy appointed course -- At no time shall ye betray thine trust -- At no time shall ye deny me - The Lord thy God - - for it is I - that hast prepared the way before thee -- So be it that I am with thee that ye might be prepared to enter into mine place of abode ---

= Watchfulness =

There are many called - - few are prepared - yet it is said: "Be ye alert and watchful - that thy foot slips not"-- Watch! be ye alert and be ye as one prepared to do battle with the forces of DARKNESS - for they sleep not - neither do they give* - - without mercy they willed the sword the sword of death - and at no time do they show mercy ---

(*retreat - weaken)

= The School of Melchezedek =

Sori Sori -- For this Word hast thou prepared thyself - and it is for the good of all that I give unto thee this part - - it shall be called: "The School of Melchezedek"- and this shall be the School of the Initiates - Not one shall enter without the proper preparation -- The preparation is that which is the "Passport" which entitles them to pass thru the portals of the School of Melchezedek --

Not one passes without the proper preparation --

It is thy part to give unto them as ye have been given to - As ye have received - so shall ye give unto them -- Their part is to receive that which is proffered -- None shall be forced - none shall be brot unprepared - neither shall preference be shown ---

= Service =

No price is placed upon their head - no price is placed upon them - - their puny penny is of no value within the School of Melchezedek - for it is earned by labor - and service to mankind - without thought of self SELFLESS service -- And no man enters herein without the qualifications - without his record which follows him where he goes - it also precedes him - for it cannot be hidden from him - neither from the Mighty Council ---

= T-M-C =

The Mighty Council admits him and prepares for the next step - his work - and for his part - his welfare - - and he has but to apply himself diligently - whole heartedly - and without thought of self ---

= Protection =

For this do I say unto thee: "Let thy foot not slip - let thy hand be mine thy words mine - - let it be that I am thy Shield and thy Buckler" ---

= Obedience =

For this do I say: "Come - follow ye me - and I shall bring thee safely". So be it and Selah ---

= For the Record =

Write ye that which I give unto thee to write - and it shall serve its purpose - - it shall not be lost to the ravages of TIME - for I shall see to that - for every word that hast been written is recorded on solid - pure golden leaves - which are placed within the secret place wherein no mortal hand might destroy --

Put thine hand in mine and I shall lead thee thru the archives of time wherein such things are to be seen and understood - wherein there is no waste or erosion --

Better shall ye understand when ye have seen these records - - better shall ye prepare thyself for thy next part ---

= Admonition =

Now ye shall do that which I give unto thee to do - and ye shall not quibble over words - neither shall ye be as one which is lacking in knowledge - - for have I not brot thee hence? Have I not given unto thee strength - and the authority to speak for me - in mine name?

Now ye shall do the things I give unto thee to do - and ye shall not fail --

Be ye as one prepared - - walk ye with surety - and ask favors of no man -- Be ye as one on whose head I place mine hand - and in whose hand thine hand rests --

Wait upon me - and serve the Light which I Am ---

= Love =

My Word is valid - and I am come that ye might have Light - that darkness be dispelled -- And at this time I would say unto thee: The way is open unto them which have the will to follow me -- There is but one way unto mine Father's place of abode - - that is Truth - and Justice which brings the other aspects -- Wherein have they been enumerated wherein have they been pointed out?

Yet I say unto the one which would follow me: Love is the secret - Love manifests itself in Truth and Justice - Mercy - and Charity --

Fail ye not in this - -

And for it is the first attribute of Love -- These attributes are but part of the One Whole of the Father - the fulfilling of the Law --

The fulfillment of the Law is LOVE - -

And for this does the Father send me - that ye might know the meaning of Love -- For this have I touched thee - - for this hast thine own heart been cleaven - - and for this hast thou sorrowed for the fallen of mankind - for the sunken - and depraved ---

= **Responsibility** =

Bless those which sorrow for them - for they shall be lifted up --

Yet I say: Ye shall not be as an ass unto them - for they shall not ride upon thy back --

They shall carry their own burdens - and make ready themself for to receive their own passport - their own inheritance --

So let them learn the way of the Initiate - the way of righteousness and all shall be well with them ---

= Victory =

This I would point out unto thee: There is one which would put within thy hand the sword of Truth - and the power to wield it - - yet that One ever knows his part - his responsibility unto himself and his station - his office -- He hast won his victory thru and by obedience unto the Law - unto the Brotherhood of the Melchezedeks ---

= The Sacrifice =

I say - this loyalty is the outcome of long training - long long experiences - which causes the candidate to bring himself unto the Altar of the Most High Living God as a living Sacrifice ---

= The Guardian =

Therein he begins his preparation for his Adeptship - his Sonship ---

He cries out for Light - that he might serve the Light - that all men might be lifted up -- And he then is heard - found - and given as it is wise and prudent -- He fares well - for as he is prepared he receives - and none are overlooked ---

For the candidate is never alone - he is accompanied by one which has been assigned unto him for the purpose of prompting him in the time of doubt - and in the time of trial ---

While he walks in silence for the most part - he is present - and for that matter he is watchful - for the enemy draws nigh unto the candidate when the victory is most won ---

= Free Spirit =

I say unto thee: Be ye mindful of thy "Guardian" and let him be unto thee thy Shield and Buckler - - for this does he walk with thee - and ye shall be as one blest to be aware of him - for he cares for thee in the hours of thy unknowing - in the hours of thy sleep -- Yet it is said - ye sleep not - for thy body of flesh sleepeth - while thy "Am" returneth unto the place of instruction - that ye be filled with knowledge and wisdom ---

= The Melchezedeks =

The School of Melchezedek is the place wherein ye are trained -- The Melchezedeks are the Ones which are trained - which have been trained for their part - - for their places differ one from the other - and yet all are part of the GREAT and DIVINE PLAN - the plan which was before the world WAS! So be it that the Melchezedeks are the Ones which are prepared to bring order out of chaos - and it shall be the Order which shall not be broken - the Order which shall be perfect - and the Order which shall withstand the destruction of man --

The destruction of man shall be as nought - for it shall be as a foul wind which shall pass before a gentle breeze -- So be it - it is decreed and prophesied aforehand -- So let it be as The Father hast willed it.

= Each unto His Part =

Wherein is it said that ye shall walk with me and talk with me -- it shall be according unto the plan - And not one shall be out of his place - not one shall be unaccounted for - for all the ones which have heard mine voice and answered me shall be as ones of mine fold - for I shall gather them in as part of the fold -- And these shall be as none other - for they shall be as ones set apart for that which they are to do - and they shall be trained in that part - and none shall trespass upon the part of the other each shall have his own part - and all parts shall fit into the Great Whole the One - - for not one shall do the work of another - each shall do his own work and know that which he is to do --

Be ye as one prepared - - for this do I call unto thee this day - that ye might come forth - - and be ye free from all bondage - from all darkness --

Know ye the true from the false - - seek ye the Truth and no harm can befall thee --

Bless thyself - as none other can bless thee - for it is given unto thee this day to choose thy way - the way ye shall go - and no man shall say unto thee nay!

= **Offspring** =

Prepare thy household that it might be in order - let thine offspring be as ones prepared that they might choose wisely -- And be ye as one responsible for the training of thy offspring - that they know the true from the false --

Pay ye no heed to the promptings of man's opinions -- Seek ye the Light - and walk ye in It fearlessly - for I have prepared before thee the Way - and ye have but to seek and ye shall find - for it is the law ---

= **The Light** =

Born of the Light art thou - born of TRUTH art thou - and ye shall come to know thy Source -- So be it The Father's Will --

Let it be known that I Am come that ye be blest - that ye be lifted up --

Let it be known that I am in the place wherein there is no darkness for the Light expels the darkness - - for the Light expands and the darkness decreases into nothing --

This is the Word I give unto them which seek the Light: The Light increases according to thy capacity to receive it - for thou art as yet not come into the fullness of thy inheritance - - thy capacity is not sufficient as yet -- For this I come that thy capacity be increased - for this hast the School of Melchezedek been established upon the Earth -- For this hast ones been sent that there be Light in the Earth ---

Never hast there been so great a stir as this day - when so many run hither and yon - seeking the way of salvation -- They know not from whence they come - neither where they goeth --

When it comes that they are called unto their places which they have prepared themself for - they shall find that they have not understood the Way of "The Lord" - they have been blinded by man's opinions and man's offal --

There are ones which have taught the teachings of the Ancients – and thot them truth - yet unto these I would say: Great hast been the changes made since the beginning of these Great and Good things which were given for their time and age - for they served well their time and peoples -

Yet - now that which was set forth in All the Great works given for man's upliftment/ enlightenment - is safeguarded - and held in trust for them which seek Truth and Light --

While the Key lies within thy hand - it is concealed from the unprepared - the eyes of the unjust and imprudent - that they might not find and misuse it for their own end --

Therefore I say unto thee: Be ye as wise - and give not thy pearls of great price unto them which would tear down and destroy --

I say: "Tear down - and destroy" for there are ones which do wear the sacred symbols - and the robes of color - that they be noticed - heard seen - and praised for their goodness and humility --

I say! Beware lest thy foot slips - for thy authority comes not thru the outer display of colors - signs and amulets ---

= **Evil** =

Listen while I tell thee of the Sorcerer's lot - Be ye as one mindful of him which sits in wait for his prey - - as the vulture he sits with bated breath - that he might bring into his lair the prey - and use him unto his own vicious end -- I say - beware the sorcerer and his partners - for they do bear witness of each other - they bear the same mark - that of the beast --

Behold ye the mark - and wait upon me that ye fall not prey unto his wiles and schemes --

Hast it not been said - that the Victor is the Victor - for his strength hast overcome the evil of the enemy - - it is so -- By his own effort shall he overcome all evil - - by his own strength shall he overcome the evils which confront him - and which shall be put in his way --

Therefore I say unto thee: Fear not - for I am come that ye have the path clearly marked - - all the pitfalls are clearly marked - - all the parts which have confronted thee shall be made clearly - and ye shall arise with honor and dignity -- So be it and Selah ---

= It is Lawful =

Wherein is it said that: "When the student is ready the Master will appear"?

Hast it not been said: "As ye are prepared so shall ye receive"? It is lawful that I say unto thee: I am come this day that all might have Light It is lawful that I say - that I Am come that they which are of a mind to follow me might be brot out of darkness --

Yet it is not lawful that I give unto the uninitiated that which they have not prepared themself for to receive -- This I too would say: That when thou hast prepared thyself for to receive me - I shall make mine self known unto thee - - and for this have I come into the Earth - that I find mine own - and that they might come to know me even as I know them --

So shall it be that these shall go where I go - and they shall be as ones prepared to do that which I do - for they shall be mine own - and they shall wear the Crown which shall be firmly placed upon their head by The Most High - and He shall bless them as none other - for He shall endow them with the power which shall be theirs to keep - - for by their own effort - obedience - and loyalty shall they prove themself TRUSTWORTH --

I am come this day that this might be so -- So be it that I have offered unto All mine hand - mine love - mine assistance -- I have said:

"Come - Come follow me "- and unto all which come I say: Be ye as ones trustworth - as ones prepared to go where I go -- Falter not - turn not thy face from me - for I shall do that which I have said I shall do - I shall not fail thee - I shall do mine part - - for this am I sent that ye be lifted up - even as I --

Let it be understood that none enter into the place wherein I abide unprepared - - none come unprepared! for I am the Gate Keeper - I am the Porter at the Gate - and none enter unaware --

I bring them which are prepared to enter herein -- I bring them even before the Throne of the Most High - and before Him - they bow unto Him in holy adoration and with praise for - unto - the Great and Grand Majesty of His Being---

= **The Holy Rites** =

They are as ones which have earned the Rites - they have been found worthy to partake of the Holy Rites of Initiation - wherein they shall be prepared to do Greater things --

They shall be blest to go where I go - and do the things I do - and they shall be as the Sons of God by Divine Rite - and no man shall take from them the power and authority to do His Will -- Therefore I say unto thee: Behold ye the Glory of The Lord thy God - and be ye as one prepared to go where He leads thee -- Fear not - for He is Sent of The Most High - Who is The Father of All - The Source of thy Being - for in Him thou art - - thou art of Him begotten

For this hast He sent me - that ye might return with me - even as ye went out --

Be ye mindful of thy Source - and fear nought - for He is thy Shield and thy Buckler ---

= **Gratitude** =

Praise ye the Name of Solen Aum Solen - - -

Sori Sori -- I say unto thee: This shall be the handbook for them which are ready to receive this mine Word - and they shall be as ones blest to receive it - - they shall be as ones prepared to receive yet Greater Light and knowledge -- Now ye shall withhold this part from them which have not had the preparation to receive - - the ones which have fallen by the way shall not be given this part - for it is not for them --

I say unto them which receive this part: Be ye as one responsible for that which ye do with it - for it is part of thy preparation for Greater responsibility -- Be ye as wise as the serpent and silent as the Sphinx.

Recorded by Sister Thedra

Councils - Schools - Brotherhood

Sori Sori -- For this time let it be done as the Father would have it be - It is given unto me to come as one Sent -- and for this have I come as one Sent -- Now ye shall put on the whole Armor of God - and ye shall be as one prepared for the part which shall be given unto thee -- Ye shall be as one which shall walk tall - and ye shall not fail - neither shall ye want -- Be ye as one blest to receive me - and ye shall be as one in whose favor I shall be - - be ye blest this day -- Accept that which I give unto thee in the name of the Father Mother Son - for it is of Him that I am Sent---

Ye shall accept this mine word - and ye shall give it unto them which await it - in the name of Our Father - Solen Aum Solen - - for this is mine word on which ye might rely - for it is valid --

Give unto me credit for knowing that which I say unto thee - for I am one of the School of Melchezedek - I am one of the Brotherhood of Melchezedek yet ye distinguish not the difference --

I say All are one under the Mighty Council - the OVER ALL Council -- Wherein is it said that the Mighty Council is the High Council under which ALL other councils function ---

Some are lesser than others - yet all who serve as the servants of the Most High are in the care and direction of the Great and Mighty Council - each having its head - each having its part within the whole - while none exist separate - and without guidance in some measure --

The Great and Mighty Council is the Source of the Light which is focused unto the lesser councils - as they are prepared to receive - each as he is capable of receiving ---

There are ones which stand with their hands before their eyes - fingers in their ears - that they hear not - nor see that which is done by these Councils of Light -- Therefore they receive lesser light - wisdom understanding - wherefore it is said: Take thine fingers out thine ears and hear that which is said - for the time is come when great Light shall be given unto the one which seeks the Light

For this do I say unto thee: Pay ye heed to that which is said - - it is said in such a manner that the uninitiated might not read the meaning thereof - that he might not see that which is hidden from the uninitiated the eyes of the profane - - I say it is hidden up from the unjust ---

They shall not see - they shall not find that which is hidden - for they would but misuse that which is revealed unto the "Initiate"---

Pay ye heed - and listen - see - and know ye that which is hidden - for this is it said: "Seek the Light - see the Light - walk ye in it" ---

Place thine own self on the altar of the Most High Living God - as a living sacrifice - - Behold ye the glory of such sacrifice - for ye shall find therein thy own self--

Behold ye all things made new -

Behold ye the Glory of God -

Behold ye the Glory of the Heaven -

Behold ye the Being which thou art -

Behold ye Me - the Light which I Am -

Behold ye the Source of Light -

For the Father Mother hast sent thee forth as part of the One -- In Him thou art staid - in Him thou hast thy being -- So be it and Selah --

Recorded by Sister Thedra

Assurance

Sori Sori -- This mine word I would give unto them which have received "The Hand Book of The Melchezedeks"- and it is for their own good that I give unto them this mine word - - for it shall be as a reminder unto them of the responsibility which goes with such as they have sought (the Knowledge of the Initiate) - the Power of the Initiate I say it is great - and for this hast it been said: "Prepare thyself for to receive"- - for this is it said: "Be ye as one trust worth"---

Now it is come when one shall try to disarm thee - when thy trials shall be as never before - and when thy friends shall forsake thee - and when thy families shall be as thy enemies - and thy strength shall avail thee nought

It is then that ye shall cry out for assistance/ for help/ for the strength which hast failed thee --

Yet I say unto thee: FEAR NOT! for thou art not alone - thou art NOT alone! For that matter there is a Mighty Host ready to assist thee Be ye as one prepared to accept that which they proffer -- So be it and Selah ---

I bring unto thee assurance that I am with thee unto the end -- So be it that I shall not forsake thee in the time of thy trials and temptation.

Be ye aware of Them - know ye that there is the Host - and one which walks by thy side - ever ready to assist - when it is wise and expedient ---

I say unto thee - be ye as one prepared - and ye shall prove thyself <u>trustworth</u>!

So be it as the Father hast willed it --

T. = Remember Jesus' initiations - -

Recommended references:- Bible - Aquarian Gospel Vale Owens' Lowlands of Heaven - Highlands of Heaven -Ministry of Heaven - Battalions of Heaven --

Recorded by Sister Thedra

Sonea - One of the Host

Sori Sori -- Long hast it been since I have spoken - yet the time is come that I shall again speak unto thee - - for it is the will of mine Father Solen Aum Solen -- For this I speak - - for this do I say unto thee: Ye shall be as one blest to receive me - and that which I have for thee -- It is for the good of all that I come this day - and it behooves me to say unto thee - that mine word is valid - and ye shall bear witness of me - and mine word ---

Let it be known that there is a Host of Mighty Enlightened Ones which serve thee - which serve the Father - for He is the Light - the Truth - the Way - and there is no other -- We of the Host bear witness of Him - for We are His Hands and feet made manifest unto thee ---

We - of the Host - have given of Ourself that ye might know - that ye might be brot out of bondage - that ye might have Light - that ye might be one of "The Host"-- So be it as The Father hast willed it ---

I come as thy Sibor - known as Sonea - as One which hast kept an eye on thy progress - and one which hast kept thee in the time of unknowing -- So be it that I am with thee - and I shall be unto thee an Elder Brother - and ye shall be as the younger brother - - for this shall I go before thee and lead the way - and no harm shall befall thee -- Ye shall walk in places strange - and far - yet I say - no harm shall befall thee --

= The Very Small Seed =

Come - Come - let us explore regions far and strange - without fear or anxiety -- There are regions strange and far - unexplored by thee - which need thee and thy assistance ---

There are ones yet unborn in flesh of Earth - which await the coming into Earth -- These are of the new generations unborn - which shall be given the assistance necessary for their coming -- These shall find a new world strange unto thee - yet the two shall be integrated as one - for this New Generation shall have their memory in part - - therefore they shall be better prepared for their new part ---

Let it be known that these things shall be done in the New Day - - The day is now come when ye shall know that all is one - - yet I say unto thee: "In mine Father's House are many Mansions" - it is true - and ye shall come to know as I know - - for thy world shall become as a Very Small Seed in the Granary of mine Father's Kingdom - - for He hast places far - and near - which thou knowest not - - far - and near - I say! for thou hast not even explored the fullness of the world at thy feet - neither above thy head -yet I say unto thee: Come - and I shall take thee farther out - where there is no darkness - no confusion - no lethargy - no sorrow - without fear - and without haste -- Come - Come and I

shall lead thee - be ye as one forewarned - forearmed - foreprepared --
-

Let it serve thee well - for I am He which stands by thee in the hours of thy unknowing ---

I Am He - - I AM HE - which is Sent --

So be it as The Father hast Willed it --

Recorded by Sister Thedra

Sori Sori -- For this have I called thee at this hour - that ye might add this unto that which hast been given unto thee for them which are prepared to receive -- So let it be for the good of all --

= **Initiation** =

This I would say that they might know - that they might be blest to know ---

There is a time of unknowing - and a time of knowing -- The time of knowing is now come - when there shall be ones prepared to receive certain truth - - certain truth which is wise to unveil at THIS time ---

There is a time to unveil certain truth - portions at a time - unto certain ones which are prepared to receive it ---

These have been called "Initiates" -- These have been initiated into the so-called "Mysteries" - and these are prepared to receive these unrevealed truths - that is - that which hast been veiled from the uninitiated ---

= **Mysteries** =

These things are no longer a mystery when revealed - - for thy unknowing - are they mysteries --

These so-called mysteries are that which is truth and law - that which operates by natural law - - and when understood there is no mystery --

This I would point out unto the ones which ask for light:--

Be ye as ones trustworth - as ones prepared to receive - for great responsibility goes with knowledge – Great responsibility goes with Gifts which are given of the Spirit

Now for this I would say unto them which ask for Gifts: Be ye aware of the responsibility which accompanies such Gifts --

For this is it said: "Prepare thyself" - "Be ye trustworth" - "Betray not thy trust - thyself" - "Put thy foot not into a hole" --

= **For This** =

For this is one sent that ye be aware of thy responsibility--

For this is one sent that ye be prepared --

For this is one sent that ye might not fall - neither shall ye fear --

For this is he thy constant companion --

For this is it said: "When the student is ready the Master will appear"-- It is So -- So be it and Selah ---

Now - I would say unto thee: Be ye sure of thy footing - - let thy feet be firmly planted -- Let thy speech be the speech of the Initiate -- Let thy hand be firmly planted in His - the One Sent - and ye shall be as one led firmly and gently - unto heights undreamed of ---

Let it be known that there are greater heights - greater attainment - greater responsibility – greater revelations - Greater Glories ---

Behold ye the Glory of the Heights!

For this have I come - that ye might attain the Heights

Recorded by Sister Thedra

Sponsors

Sori Sori--

Be it expedient that I say unto thee this day - that the way is made clear before thee - and it behooves thee to go before them - as I have gone before thee - for they shall be as the younger brothers which are to follow --

I say they - the younger brothers which shall follow thee shall be as the "porters at the gate" for the ones which are yet unborn --

They shall stand sponsor for the ones to follow after them -- It is the law: As one is "raised up" he gives assistance unto them which come after them - - Therefore it is said: "Be ye as one prepared for that which ye are to do"--

Give unto me thine hand - and I shall put into it a plan - and it shall serve thee well - and ye shall not fail --

Be ye faithful unto thy trust - betray not thyself - and give unto me credit for knowing that which I say unto thee -- Fear not - hold ye steadfast - - Give unto the Source of thy Being credit for thy Being - - praise ye the name of Solen Aum Solen --

Harken unto mine voice - and be ye as one responsible for that which is given unto thee to do -- Wear ye the Royal Robe with dignity and with power - the power which is endowed unto thee of the Father Mother God - and ye shall be as a Son of God --

Let thine light so shine that others might know that ye are as a Son which hast the Seal upon thy forehead - for they shall see it - and they shall be as ones which find thee - - by thy own light shall they be drawn unto thee -- They shall be as the ones seeking Light - and ye shall give unto them assistance - even as I assist thee --

Be ye as the forerunner of me - for ye shall prepare them to receive me - - for is it not said: “Ye go before me to prepare the way for my coming"--

I have gone before thee that ye might find thy way back unto thy Source - - now ye are to prepare them that they might receive me - even as thou hast received me - - and they shall come to know me even as ye know me -- So be it and Selah --

Recorded by Sister Thedra

The Covenant

Sori Sori -- For this hour let this be done according unto mine Father's Will - and it shall be for the good of all mankind -- So let it be -- Amen and Selah --

Be ye as one which hast the will to do that which shall be given unto thee to do - and ye shall not want - neither shall ye fail --

This I would say unto thee: Be ye as one prepared to go forth as a bride adorned to meet her bridegroom - for he cometh - and he approaches swiftly - and surely --

The bridegroom cometh as "One Sent"- and ye shall accept him as One Sent of the Father - for such he is - - and he shall claim thee as His Own - and no man shall say unto Him - nay!

Be ye as one blest to receive Him - for he is the Son of the Most High Living God --

Blest shall ye be - for he shall take thee as a bride which is prepared to receive her bridegroom --

Blest shall ye be - for ye shall abide with him as one wed unto him and ye shall not be found wanting --

While it is said - thy work hast but begun - I say: Greater things shall ye do - for ye shall walk knowingly - ye shall be as one on whose shoulders I place mine mantle - and I shall give unto thee a plan which shall be the Covenant twixt them and me - and no man shall turn thee aside - neither shall he deter thee from thy course --

Be ye as one which hast covenanted with me - - remember thy covenant - made so long ago - - for this shall be revealed unto thee - - for this do I say: "Remember"- for this I say: "Be as one prepared"--

By thine own hand shall I lead thee -- By thine own will shall ye follow where I lead thee -- By thine own light shall thy way be made smooth --

Sori Sori -- For this hour I say hear ye me - - And know ye that I am He which is come - that ye be brot out of bondage -- For this have I quickened thee - and it shall be for the good of All - that I bring thee forth - that they too might be quickened --

Let them which have ears hear that which I say unto thee - for it shall profit them --

Withhold not this mine word from them - for it shall be as mine word unto them - that they might know me - even as ye know me -- So be it as the Father hast willed --

Bear ye witness of me - carry high mine banner - bear ye the name which I have given unto thee - - let all men adore the name which I have given unto thee mine own --

Retreat not - for I say: The dragon shall approach thee as one which has the power to attack - - yet he shall not overcome thee - for I am with thee unto the end --

Be ye not fearful - for I shall be thy Shield and thy Buckler - - I shall not forsake thee in thy hour of trial --

Hast it not been said: "I Am thy Shield and thy Buckler"- I Am He which stands porter at the gate - that no evil befall thee -- I AM HE - Sent - that ye might not fail -- So be it and Selah --

Recorded by Sister Thedra

Sori Sori -- So be it that there is one which hast his hand upon thee - and he hast come unto thee at this hour - that ye might receive of him this word - which shall be a light unto the feet of the novice --

= The Constant Companion =

The Light which shall fall upon the feet of the novice - shall be from the lamp which He carries - - he goes before the novice that he might lead him safely into the Inner Temple - wherein he might find his own light --

= In His Footsteps =

I say unto thee: I am come that ye might be safe-guarded thru thy hours of trial and temptations - - lead thou - as I have led thee - and be ye as one on whose shoulders rests great responsibility --

= Preparation =

For this have I directed thee - for this have I sponsored thee - and it is now come when ye shall lead them - even as I have led thee -- So be it and Selah -- Therefore - I say unto thee: Be ye as one come alive - and ye shall walk knowingly - - ye shall know as I know - and ye shall not fail - neither shall ye want --

= The Light unto My Feet =

Mine lamp is trimmed and burning - it is the Light by which ye find thy way thru the shadows - the deep and dark shadows - which haunt the one which aspires to attain the height Feign not wisdom - for wisdom is that which is to be the reward of the Victor - - the victory won - wisdom attained -- Let it be remembered that the wise one leads on - - the neophyte follows willingly --

This I would point out: There is none which bring thee against thy will - none to carry thee on their back -- Ye shall follow of thy own free will and strength -- Hear ye - and remember that which is said -- bear ye witness of me - and fear not - for I am with thee - and I shall not forsake thee -- Place thy hand firmly in mine - and I shall lead thee aright --

Forget not - that I am he which is Sent that ye be safeguarded thru the darkness - and my Light shall not fail thee -- Be ye responsive unto mine Voice - for I say: "Come - follow where I lead thee - and ye shall not fail"--

Recorded by Sister Thedra

= The Word of The Lord =

Sori Sori -- Let thine hand be mine hand - and ye shall give unto them which are prepared to receive - this mine word - for it shall profit them. This mine word is given unto them for their own sake - that they might know that which is given unto them this day -- So be it and Selah ---

= The Ages =

This day is a new day - and each has its place - its time - its part - - and all fits into the age - past - present and future --

The law is such that each day brings its own fulfillment - as does each age - - the age is but the many days - such as the weeks become years ---

= The Purpose =

Now I say - that ye are now come into this age for a divine purpose - that of fulfilling a law - the law under which ye come -- This law hast been given names varyingly - and names which are not always correct.

= Its Not the End =

These are the days which have been foretold long ago - in ages past - - yet it is not the end of all the world - neither of the Earth - for I say unto thee: The Earth shall not perish! Neither shall She be finished in this Age - for She shall be delivered!

= Suffering =

This I would say - that there shall be trials and suffering - and there shall be wailing and cries for peace - - yet no peace shall be found within their plans - for they are not of a mind to accept peace --

= Futility =

Peace is not within them - they are of the mind to serve the dragon - - therefore I shall withdraw mine hand from them and they shall perish -

they shall learn well their lesson - - from their lessons shall they learn the way of peace - and the futility of war --

= A Lesson Learned =

So be it that they shall at last come to know the meaning of "Brotherhood"- the meaning of "Love ye one another"--

= Self Assurance =

Now for this day - I would speak unto thee - that ye might not suffer for them - or wait with them - - yet ye shall be mindful of their suffering --

= Atonement =

They shall be responsible for their own “sins" - - There shall be no place to hide - no cover for their nakedness - they shall stand naked before me - the Lord thy God -- They shall be weighed in the balance - and be found wanting

= Warning =

I say: The law hast been given - the law in its simplicity hast been made clear - that even the simple might understand.

= God's Grace =

Wherein is it said that - "Fools shall be raised up to do the Will of the Father which hast Sent me"- it is so - - and these shall be glorified above all the great and glorified of the Earth - which are as traitors unto their trust

= Messengers =

There are ones sent even as I - that they be warned of the dangers which lie ahead - - while they go headlong into battle - crying for blood -- I say unto them: "Lay down thy arms - and know ye that ye are brothers flesh of one flesh - brothers all - and ye hear me not!!"--

= I Am Come =

This is the day of reckoning! I am Come! - That the Age be as none other -- I am Come that they might have Light - that they perish not --

= Voice in the Wilderness =

For this is given unto me - that they might be delivered of their own bondage -- While they turn from me and mine word - I am helpless to give unto them mine assistance -- I am come crying: "Awaken ye children of Earth! Awaken all ye nations of the Earth!"- Yet they heed not mine Voice - they turn a deaf ear unto me ---

= The Wicked =

Now I shall do that which I am to do - I shall withdraw mine hand - and they shall go the way of flesh - - and ye shall not grieve for them - for they shall be as ones prepared in the place wherein they shall go - for that which shall be given unto them to do --

= Slaughter =

They shall see the folly of their ways - they shall find therein the foolishness of sacrifice unto me - the futility of slaughter - hatred – envy.

= Sacrifice =

They shall know that the only profitable sacrifice is "Self" - and self-sacrifice is the only sacrifice acceptable unto the Father which hast Sent me --

= The Law =

They shall turn unto the Light crying for assistance - then they shall be heard and answered -- So be it as the law asks judgement - it is accorded as they are prepared to receive - - Justice rendered I say! for the Law is just!!

= Servants & Traitors =

This I would say unto thee: Serve ye the Light - which I Am - - Serve ye selflessly - and with all thy heart - giving unto me credit for being that which I am -- Know ye that I am come that All men be lifted up -- Yet I say: I am as one rejected by the traitors - and I find they are a rebellious lot - and they are as ones which have thrown over their own life belt --

= Deliverance =

They shall cry out - and they shall find no place of safety save in me -- They shall at last turn unto the Light and call - and then they shall find that the Light shall not fail them which seek - - They shall then be delivered from their bondage -- This is - "Repentance -- Blest are they which turn unto the Light - - Blest are they which seek the Light - which I Am --

Recorded by Sister Thedra

Greater Things Shall Ye Do

Sori Sori -- This is mine time with thee - and ye shall be as one prepared to enter into the Inner Temple wherein I abide - - for this have I brot thee hence - - for this have I said: "Follow thou me"- for this have I led thee hither --

I bring thee into the place wherein ye are prepared to go -- I bring thee into the places wherein ye go - that ye be prepared for the Inner Temple wherein I abide –

= The Greater Capacity =

This I have said unto thee: "As ye prepare thyself - so shall ye receive"- Now I say: Thy time is come when ye shall be as one prepared for Greater things - and ye shall walk with me - counsel with me - and do that which I shall give unto thee to do --

Ye shall know well thy part - and ye shall not fail -- Ye shall bring them forth as ones prepared - - ye shall bring them in as the harvest - - ye shall find them which have gone astray - and ye shall prepare them even as thou hast been prepared --

Thy harvest shall be great - for the time is come when they shall come seeking the Light - - and ye shall find them ready to receive that which I have given unto thee for them -- So be it I shall bring them unto thee - and they shall heed that which ye say unto them --

They shall give heed unto thee - and they shall be as ones blest to heed -- Be ye as one blest - for ye shall not fail --

= Assurance =

Ye shall stand firm - and walk ye tall - - for I say unto thee: Mine hand is upon thee - and ye shall be as one in authority - for I have called thee forth and given unto thee the power and authority to speak in mine name - that which I give unto thee to say ---

= The Greater Sight =

Now it is come when ye shall see the plan set before thee -- There is a plan - which thou hast seen in part only - - yet thou shall see in Greater measure - and ye shall rejoice that ye have been given the Gift of Sight.

There is one which shall come unto thee - and he shall have within his hand the power and the authority to give unto thee that Gift of Sight --

= Responsibility =

Ye shall accept it in the name of the Father which hast Sent me -- Ye shall be as one on whose shoulders rests Great responsibility - for it brings with it (the Gift) Greater responsibility --

While I say: "it brings greater responsibility" - I have said: "As ye are prepared - so shall ye receive"--

Ye shall now go forth as one prepared for that responsibility ---

= Admonition =

Let not thy foot slip - for it is mine part to go before thee - that the way be prepared before thee - - and it is thy part to follow where I lead thee. So be it I say: "Come - follow ye me - the way I have prepared before thee"

Make strait the way of the Lord - and ye shall find that I have made the way before thee strait and accessible unto thee ---

= Temple of Charity =

It is now come when we have entered into the Temple of Charity - and therein ye shall find many which shall be unto thee great Light -- Ye shall be given instruction in the way of the Initiate - and ye shall know that which ye shall do - - and ye shall go forth renewed - as one prepared to enter into the next door which shall open before thee - - for it shall be as the open door before thee - and ye shall pass as one prepared --

I say: "Pass ye in"

So be it and Selah

Recorded by Sister Thedra

= The Time of Need =

Sori Sori --

Say unto them in mine name - that the time cometh swiftly - when they shall stand as ones shorn of all their vainglory - all their pride - all their selfishness --

They shall stand humbled before the Lord of Lords - - they shall be as little children - helpless - crying for bread - - for they shall be in need.

I say: "They shall be in need!"- for they have set into motion that which shall be unto them their undoing - so be it the law - - they shall reap what they have sown --

Be ye as mine mouth - mine Voice unto them - and give unto them this mine word -- I say: "They shall be in need!" - for they have turned their face from me - their Benefactor--

They have discredited me - and mine word - - they have been as the traitor unto themself - while I stand before them with hands outstretched --

They have rushed headlong into the pit -- They have been as ones prone to destruction -- They have fashioned for themself their own pit. They have given unto themself credit for being wise --

Let it suffice that I say unto them: "Turn from the way of war - seek ye the Light - which I Am - and be ye as ones prepared that I might enter in"--

Wherein is it said - that they have turned me out - shut the door in mine face - blasphemed the Name of the Father Which hast Sent me --

So be it that they shall come to know that which they do is the way of the dragon -- They shall turn from him and seek the Light - they shall stand as ones in need - - so be it I shall give unto them as they are prepared to receive

Let it profit them to turn from their way - and seek the Light - which shall be unto them Peace - - Peace shall be established within them - - and they shall war no more --

For this do I stand by - ready to give assistance - and be unto them their assistant in the time of need -- Wait upon me in the time of thine youth - and I shall remember thee in thine old age --

Wherein is it said that - "They shall come unto me with clean hands"- - I say: "They shall lay down their arms - and be as ones prepared to accept me"- they shall be as ones prepared!

They shall be as ones on whose shoulders rests the responsibility of their own mis-used energy - their own "Sins"-- Let it be according unto the LAW --

While I say - they shall stand as ones humble before me - I say: They shall come as little children crying for bread - asking for sustenance of me -- then I shall give unto them as they are prepared to receive --

While I now say: They shall stand as ones shorn of their power - of their glory - vainglory - conceit - their boastings - - their aggression shall profit them nought - for they shall be brot low --

Bear ye in mind that there is no hiding place - no place can they hide from me - from the Father Which hast given them Life! They shall come to know that I Am He which is Sent that they might find Peace - Peace Eternal --

I say unto them: Turn from thy way - seek the Light - lay down thy arms - and give unto me credit for knowing that which I say unto thee.

Cast aside thy plans of aggression - and be ye as ones prepared for Peace -- I bring not Peace - - I bring unto thee a Plan - that Peace be established within thy heart --

Wait upon ME - serve ye the Light - and be ye as ones blest of Me for I am come that ye be blest -- For this do I say: "Come as one prepared to receive Me". For this do I reveal mineself at this time -- Behold ye the Glory of the "Lord"- for He hast spoken that ye be blest Behold ye the Way of Peace - - Behold ye the way of destruction!

For it lies before thee! I say: "Turn ye and be ye as ones alert unto Mine Word -- Heed that which I say -- PERISH NOT! WANT NOT!"

Recorded by Sister Thedra

=His will Made Manifest =

Sori Sori --

Be ye as one blest to receive of me - this my Word - - record it for them - that they might be prepared to receive me in the name of Mine Father which hast sent me --

As His Will I come - for I am His Will made manifest -- It is now come when ye shall go forth - and ye shall do that which I give unto thee to do - and ye shall not falter - or fail --

Ye shall walk fearlessly - and with surety -- ye shall do that which I give unto thee to do - and ye shall be as mine hand and foot made manifest --

For this have I prepared thee -- Ye shall bring them into the place which I have prepared for them - - and as they have prepared themself so shall they receive --

It is said: They shall choose where they go - yet it is said: They prepare themself for the place they shall go - they shall be put into the place they belong -- Each shall be in his proper environment - for he shall be in like company --

I say unto them: "Seek ye the Light" - and they shall find--

They shall first make ready themself -- They shall put from themself all pettiness/ childishness/ foolishness/ and they shall be as ones which are prepared to receive me - <u>then</u> I shall touch them - and give unto them in capacity as they are able to receive --

It is said: Come as an empty vessel - - they come - bringing their own cups - filled with the offal of their own - - their cups are filled - that no more can they contain - they are as the sealed vessel -- I cannot put 'new wine in the old cup' for it is not of the same vintage --

The opinions of man hast been unto him his own - not mine -- I say I am not of his making - of his "Vintage" - of his imaging - - he hast had many visions of me -- Many concepts hast he had - yet he hast not known me as I Am - for I am not limited as <u>man</u> - - I Am free - "FREE" I say!

Man would limit me - like unto himself - for he walks as one limited for he knows not that he is free - he hast not as yet awakened - he is as one sleeping - - yet he shall come forth as one awake - he shall walk free - as one unbound - - for this do I say - Awaken!

I come that he awaken -- So be it he shall hear me - and bestir himself - and he shall grow in strength and stature - he shall become of age - and then he shall receive of me his part - which hast been held in trust for him - until he hast reached maturity --

Man - as such is mature - - the un-mature is as the child - therefore I say: "Mine children Awaken!" and be ye blest that ye be among the Awakened -- So be it and Selah --

Let them come - let them be as the ones which have the will to learn hear - see - and receive -- Let them put their hand to the plow - - let them earn their passport - let them prove themself - then I shall do mine part --

They shall come as a little child - as one asking for bread -- They shall be as one humbled - shorn of all self-glory - they shall know themself to be in need -

They shall be in want - - They shall be as ones serviceable in Mine House - for I say: I set up Mine House in Mine Father's name - and it is in His Name that I come - - and I say: No laggards shall dwell in the House of the Lord --

Neither shall a liar - a thief - a deceiver - a tattler nor a hypocrite dwell therein --

I say: They shall be as one prepared to dwell in the House of the Lord --

They shall be as ones responsible for the part given unto them -- They shall be as ones which are prepared for a part - and it shall be given - and accepted - with gratitude and joy - - it shall be done according to the best of their ability - and they shall be obedient unto the law - which is just --

They shall waver not concerning their preparation - they shall at all times be as ones responsible for their own actions - and deeds - words and the results thereof --

They shall walk upright - knowing they are as ones responsible - knowing that I am the Master - that I am Sent that they have Light - - that I have declared unto them the LAW - - that I have set up mine Shield and Banner - under which they shall serve with honor and dignity --

I say: They shall honor mine Servants - mine Priests - mine Priestesses - Prophets - and Ambassadors - - for these I have sent unto thee that ye be lifted up -- Ye shall honor them - and be likewise honored for thy trust-worthiness -- So be it that ye shall be as one remembered - and numbered - and ye shall be as one acceptable and useful in Mine House --

So be it I say: Prepare thyself - that ye might enter into the Inner Temple wherein I abide -- So be it and Selah --

Now I say unto thee: Ye shall enter into the place wherein ye shall go - - as the outer temple - as the entrance of mine Temple is hidden from the outer temple - first ye pass the outer before ye might see the Inner --

The inner is forbidden unto thee - before ye have passed within the portals of the outer - - therefore I say: Prepare thyself for to enter into mine place of abode --

Ye shall learn obedience and Love - then ye shall be as one prepared to serve Me with all thy strength - all thy heart and mind -- Now ye shall place thine hand in mine - and I shall lead thee safely and with surety --

Be ye as one blest to learn well thy lessons - - and praise ye the Name of Solen Aum Solen - for He is the cause of thy being --

Let thy hand be mine - thy foot be mine - thy VOICE MINE - and ye shall be blest of Him which is The Father Eternal --

Holy - Holy - is His Name - and none other shall be glorified - none other above Him - neither below - - None other - I SAY!

Falter not - - put not thy foot into a hole - for there are many pitfalls many temptations -- Be ye alert - watchful - and remember - I am with thee - -

I am He which is Sent - -

So be it I am the Gatekeeper - -

I am the Porter at the Gate --

Recorded by Sister Thedra

= Tests =

Sori Sori --

Bear in mind that which I have said - and remember well that which I have given unto thee - for it is thy Shield and thy Buckler --

THE WORD is given unto thee that ye might be sustained in the hour of thy struggle - in the hour of thy trials and tests --

Tested ye shall be - - trials ye shall have - and ye shall be as ones blest to remember well that which hast been given unto thee ---

Fear not - for I have said unto thee: I am with thee - - ye have but to remember that which I have said - and hold high thy head - - walk ye with surety of purpose --

Praise ye the Name of Solen Aum Solen - - Know ye that nought of harm can come nigh unto thee - for I am come that ye be lifted up -- So be it and Selah ---

Return unto me that which I have given unto thee - and I shall give unto thee in greater measure - for greater Gifts have I for thee - GREATER Gifts I say - have I kept for thee - - and ye shall find that which I have kept for thee shall surpass anything thou hast ever imaged.

Thy Gifts shall be as the Stars in thy Crown - each shall be different from the others - and ye shall be as one prepared to receive these Gifts for none other shall receive them ---

Now ye shall be as one which has the power and the authority to go into the Inner Temple - the Holy of Holies - to go where I go - - and nothing shall be hidden from thee - for ye shall be as a "Son of the Living God"- and He - the Father - shall place upon thy brow the Crown of the Victor -- So be it and Selah --

Fortune thyself the Crown of Victory - return ye unto thy place of going out - receive thy Crown of the Father - and be ye as one which hast returned Victoriously -- Let it be as the Father hast willed it ---

= The Lost =

This I would say unto thee: There is not one amongst thee that hast been forgotten - - yet there are as ones which have wandered in the wilderness as ones lost - they have lost their way - they cry: "Which way - which way - which way" - for they fear - and pay no heed unto the Voice which cries: "COME - Come unto Me and be ye as one blest. Come unto Me and find peace"---

= The Way of the Dragon =

They turn unto the ways of the dragon - they ask of the sooth-sayers - they seek the necromancers - the astrologers - the numerologers - the magician and the many which trade in men's souls - - the ones who traffic in black magic --

Pity! Pity I say - - and they know not that they are trapt - they know not that which they do -- So be it I say: They shall first turn from them and seek the Light - for the Light which I Am shall be unto them their salvation -- Therefore - it behooves me to say unto them which seek the Light: "Be ye as one aware - be ye alert - put thy foot not in a hole - lest thou be entrapt"--

Seek ye first the Light and ye shall find - - seek ye the way unto the Father's House -- Be ye blest to find - - for this have I come - that ye might find thy way - that ye might return with me -- So be it as the Father hast willed it -- Amen and Selah --

Recorded by Sister Thedra

The Harvest

Sori Sori --

Bear in mind that the time is now come when man shall now be as fortuned that which they have prepared for themself - they shall now be as ones which gather their harvest - - for it is said: "As ye have sown so shall ye reap"- - there is the season of sowing past - now is the season of reaping --

This season is upon them -- It is said that they have prepared their own cup for themself - yet they proffer it unto their brother - - and they cry for peace? Wherein have they given the cup of peace? Wherein have they been at peace within themself?

= **Bitter Cup** =

Let it be as they have prepared themself - - they have prepared for themself the cup of bitters - - let them partake - and they shall drink the last bitter dreg -- And when they have drunken thereof - they shall find it bitter - THEN - they shall prepare the cup of oil - which shall serve as the healing balm for their wounds -- Then they shall turn unto the Light for their help - and they shall be given in accord to their capacity.

= **Results** =

Call it the law - call it what ye will - for it is the law - - as ye are prepared so shall ye receive -- Let not thy hand slip - neither thy tongue nor thy foot --

While I say ye shall not let thy hand slip - neither thy tongue - it is given unto me to see them giving a hand unto the enemy - - they give comfort unto the enemy - - they go forth to do a good deed - and put their foot in a hole - and find themself entrapt - - I say "entrapt" for they have prepared for themself the trap - they have spoken words which were not of me - and they have falsified that which I have said - they have misused mine words to their own end --

= **False Teachers** =

They have put words into mine mouth - which I spit out - for I say unto them: I do not give unto thee power to put words into mine mouth - neither do I give unto them power to speak for me - for they are betrayers - - they are not of me - they are not the fruit of mine labors - nor are they of mine flock --

They are of the damned - they are of the evil one - which hast betrayed himself - they follow him - THEY plan the wars --

= **Self Glory** =

They give of themself that they be satisfied - they gratify themself with blood - hatred and death - - I say - death! Yea - they are the father of destruction - they plan destruction - they are as ones which have planned the destruction of All which serve the Light --

= **Alertness** =

Be ye - O Mine Children - ever watchful - ever alert! on guard that ye put not thy foot into their trap -- Remember that I am thy Shield and thy Buckler -- I am He which is Sent to deliver thee out -- Give the enemy no footing - no power over thee and I shall do mine part - - I shall sustain thee in the hour of trials and temptations -- So be it and Selah ---

= Worthiness =

Be ye as one trust worth - betray not thyself - for it is given unto me to see them falter - and fall by the way -- They weary of mine sayings - and they fear for themself - - they faint by the way - and no heed do they give unto the WORD which I give unto them - - they think themself wise --

Yet I say: THEY HAVE BETRAYED THEMSELF

They have closed Me out

Now I say they shall wait --

= The Reward =

Blest is he which comes this day -- Blest is he which goes where I go - and he shall find favor with me -- He shall be blest as none other -- So be it and Selah --

Recorded by Sister Thedra

= Watch! =

Sori Sori --

Be ye as the hand of me - and record that which I say unto thee - - for they shall bear witness of mine words - and it shall profit them --

Say unto them in mine name - that they shall see their towers topple their ships shall rust in their berths - their guns shall sit as reminders of their foolishness - and they shall find that their machines of the air shall be as the poor part of travel - for they shall fail them - - they shall be as ones helpless - and know not which way to turn - - they shall find with all their getting - they have not gotten wisdom --

Now there shall be a great cry go up - and it shall reverberate thruout the land - and it shall be as nothing heard before - it shall be as the cry in the night --

Their places shall be as ones poured over by the enemy - - they shall be over-run - and it shall be as nothing seen before - it shall be the sign of the times --

For the enemy shall over-run the land - and he shall be as the enemy therefore it is said: Prepare thyself - PREPARE thyself!! - For the time is come when ye shall see that the enemy is not to be satisfied - he is the ENEMY - and not to be reconciled! He hast the will to destroy - lay waste - and put asunder the Rites and the Truth of man - as given of the Mighty Council --

He hast gone so far as to bring bloodshed of the little ones - to make lawful the slaughter of the unborn - - the war in which men are slain is honorable by comparison -- I say: It is the dragon abroad in the land -- See ye that which he does - and bear in mind that he is the evil one - the evil which is the oppressor - which holds man bound - and which is the enemy!

Dare ye stand up and be counted - for I say unto thee: Hold ye steadfast and know that I am not to be turned aside - I am with thee to the end - for ye shall stand with me in this - and I shall shield thee --

I say: TURN NOT FROM ME - FOR I AM THY SHIELD AND THY BUCKLER --

I Am that I Am -

Recorded by Sister Thedra

= Implementation =

Sori Sori --

Be ye as the hand made manifest for this part which I shall give unto them which are prepared to receive it --

Let them know that which I say unto them by this means -- I say - it is for their own good that I speak out this day - - yet they are not about the Father's business as I am - and they heed not the Voice which cries out unto them

= Where Lord? =

While it is said that they shall heed - and they shall be brot up short - - they have turned from me - seeking signs and wonders of men - asking of them peace! - - and they know not that peace is not to be found at their council tables --

They cry: "Peace - Peace - Peace"- yet they are not at peace - - peace is not in them - they have not followed in the way of PEACE --

= The Boomerang =

It is now come when the greatest of all suffering shall come upon the nations and the peoples - for they have set into motion the energy - and that which they have set into motion shall rebound upon them - - they shall be as ones on whose shoulders rests the responsibility of their own actions -- Many shall suffer the consequences of their own "Sins" - their own ways ---

And there shall be children yet unborn - which shall suffer from their deeds - so wontonly committed -- They shall be as the innocent - yet their day shall bring forth fruit which shall be sweet in their stomach - they shall eat thereof and find it sweet ---

= 666 vs O =

From this time forward it shall be given unto thee to see them yield unto the cry for blood - and they shall yield unto the cry as never before Ones shall rush headlong into the streets in frenzied passion - seeking blood -- They shall run as mad men - and they shall not be satisfied - for there shall be no satisfaction to be found in their hatred -- In their way - in their "hours" of terror they shall destroy themself - - the way in which they go shall be the way of darkness and destruction --

They shall be as ones responsible for that which they do - for I have warned them - - for ages past I have sent mine Emissaries - mine prophets - mine Messengers amongst them as mine Voice - mine feet made manifest upon the Earth - - And they have heeded not the Voice - the Word - - They have slain the prophets - the messengers - - and Emissaries have been slain - persecuted - ridiculed - and turned out - - they have been as outcasts --

= **The Traitors** =

They have given unto them the cup of gall - and found that they themselves have to drink of the cup which they have given unto the prophets and messengers and emissaries --

Poor are they - - with all their knowledge they have not been "Wise" they have boasted - and strutted before men - and they have given unto me no credit for being the "Head of State"- the Counselor - for they have not taken my Counsel --

They have not heeded my Counsel - neither have they accepted ME as their "Head of State" -- I have said: "I am the Founder of this land of Liberty" - and I have brot forth a Great Nation --

= **The House Divided** =

It is said: "In God We Trust" - yet wherein have they given unto Me the credit - the Power the Glory?

Wherein do they sing the songs of Praise unto the Lord? and wherein do they say: "Give us Liberty or give us death?

Now they shall find that they have portioned out the bitter cup for themself - the which they shall drink - and they shall find it bitter indeed. Indeed I say: IT SHALL BE BITTER!! So be it the law is exacting - "The way of sin is death"--

I am come as One Sent - crying: "Come ye out from among them - Come ye - follow me - and be ye not part of them"- yet they follow after the one which would lead them down to destruction --

While I say: "they follow the dark one - which would lead them down unto destruction" - I say they have the choice which way they go.

= Which Way? =

They which follow him willingly shall perish - - they which turn from him shall find peace -- Yet I say - the way of peace is not to be found in flesh - for flesh is not the way of peace --

Peace I give unto them which follow me - - and I say I shall return unto mine place of abode in peace - and nought of darkness shall there be wherein I go -- I am He which is come that they be delivered from bondage - and that they might know PEACE --

They shall choose this day which way they go -- So be it I have spoken and I have been heard by some - - some have given unto me credit for being that which I Am - - others have set foot against me and closed the door that I might not enter in -- Unto these I say: "The way of the rebellious is hard indeed - the way of the wonton is destruction".

= Peace =

Blest are the ones which walk with me - and serve the Light - which are mine servants - - I say: "Blest are Mine Servants for they shall be blest of Mine Father which hast Sent Me -- So be it and Selah -- Praise ye the Name of Solen Aum Solen - Unto Him ALL THE PRAISE AND THE GLORY!!

So let it be forever and forever -

Recorded by Sister Thedra

= Memory =

Be ye as one on whose head I place mine hand - and be ye blest of me and by me -- Let thy hand be mine hand - and ye shall record that which I say unto thee - and it shall serve the purpose for which it is recorded.

So be it that the time is come when ye shall do the work which I do. Ye shall go where I send thee - ye shall say that which I give unto thee to say - and ye shall know that which ye do to be that which is Mine work --

Pay ye heed unto that which I say - and be ye obedient unto that which I give unto thee - for it shall be according to the law --The law is just - and according to thy preparation so shall ye receive -- So be it and Selah ---

= Fear Not =

Fret not over thy part - for it shall be given unto thee to know that which ye are to do - that which ye have done - - and thy memory shall be restored unto thee - and ye shall remember that which is done in the hours of thy sleep - for ye shall have the memory of thy time with me - Is it not said - that - thy memory shall be restored - it is so -- So let it be as the Father wills it - - for this do I say: "Follow Me - fear not for I shall lead thee safely"--

= The Initiate =

Now I say unto thee: Bring thyself - and I shall accept thee as the sacrificial offering - - I shall give unto thee as I have received -- Ye shall be blest as I have been blest - - ye shall walk with surety - knowingly ---

Ye shall ponder mine words - and ye shall not fail -- Place thy hand in mine and I shall take thee thru the shadows safely - and then ye shall do as I have done - - ye shall assist others which follow after thee - - for this have I given unto thee assistance -- So be it - as ye receive so shall ye give - let it be - - for this do I give unto thee mine Mantle --

The Mantle of Gold I shall place upon thy shoulders - and ye shall wear it becomingly and knowingly -- Ye shall be as one on whose head rests the Crown of the Sun - and ye shall be as one prepared for the Greater part - - ye shall do greater things than thou hast dreamed of -- Ye shall stand tall - walk with surety - and go where I lead thee -- Ye shall heal the sick in mine name - and ye shall give unto the Father all the Praise and the Glory -- So be it and Selah --

= Clean the Cup =

Put aside all thy puny ideas - concepts of me - and the part which hast been given unto thee - and know ye that Greater work shall ye do - Greater things than these shall ye do - for it is needful that ye be brot out of darkness—No more shall ye walk blindly - no more shall ye wander in darkness - no more shall ye weary - no more shall ye want - So be it I have spoken and I am speaking - and I am not finished - - I shall speak again and again -- So be it and Selah --

Recorded by Sister Thedra

= The Messenger =

Sori Sori -- Be ye as mine hand made manifest unto them which have the will to follow me - the way I go --

Be ye as one blest to receive this mine word for them - - let it be recorded as I give it unto thee - and it shall be unto them much Light.

= The Message =

When they have accepted that which I have given unto them - and when they have done that which I have given unto them to do - they shall find that I am prepared to give unto them in greater measure --

= The Work Goes On =

They shall be as ones prepared to receive in greater capacity - for it shall be increased in great proportions -- None shall gainsay mine word for there is a Host which shall bear witness of mine Word - and that which I now do - - that which I have done - - and I say: I am but begun for I shall show mine hand unto them which follow where I lead them. So be it and Selah ---

= ? ? ? =

Wherein have I failed thee? Wherein hast it been given unto me to be found wanting? Wherein hast it been given unto me to be found sleeping?

= Reality =

When they awaken unto me - they shall know that I am present - that I am here - that I am not afar off in a corner -- I am not limited to any place - be it in the world of man - planet or galaxy - - I am free --

= Freedom =

It is said: Prepare thyself to go where I go - prepare thyself to do that which I do - and ye shall be free as I am free --

Freedom! Freedom! is that which is earned - "EARNED!" I say -- Thy Victory is thy Freedom --

= The Way =

Hast it not been said: This is thy concern? Hast it not been said - service is thy part? Serve Me - and thy life shall be secure - for I AM the Life the Light - - this is the WAY ---

= The Oneness =

Wherein is it said: "Be ye as mine hand and foot made manifest"- - it behooves me to say: "As ye serve ME so do ye serve the Father which hast given unto thee being --

= Awareness =

Be ye mindful of Him - and ye shall bless thyself in the remembrance of Him - - Praise ye the Name of Solen Aum Solen ---

= The Detours =

While ye shall be as one prepared to follow me - I say: ye have been as ones long on thy return - and ye have been as wanderers in the valley of despair - and ye have been as ones walking in darkness - - ye have dragged thy legirons with thee - and now ye shall lay aside thy legirons/ thy possessions - yea - even thy opinions which hast been unto thee as an unopened book - - they have not been the 'open book'- for they have been opinions - not revelations --

= The Empty Cup =

While I say: Put aside all thy preconceived opinions of me and about me - I say - Come - prove me for what I Am -- See me - Know me - walk with me - and I shall give thee comprehension -- I shall open up thine eyes - and ye shall see! and Know --

= Try Me! =

For this do I say: "Come"- for this do I say: "Walk ye with me - test me try me - and ye shall come of thy own free will"-- So let it be --

Recorded by Sister Thedra

= The Pronouncement =

Sori Sori -- Mine hand I place upon thy head and I pronounce the Word and ye receive the word in the name of the Father - the Son - and the Spirit --

The Spirit in which it is given is the Spirit in which ye receive the Word -- The Holy Spirit in which I come unto thee is the Spirit in which ye have thy being --

The Holy Spirit is that which animates the physical body with which ye now record the Word which I give unto thee --

= Discipline =

It is for thy sake that I say unto thee: Awaken and record that which I say -- "Bear ye witness of that which I say" - it is for thy own sake that I call thee at this hour (2:45 am) when ye obey mine touch--

Ye have been alert unto the touch and responded promptly -- Now I say unto thee: Ye shall have greater responsibility - for I shall require of thee Greater Service - Greater responsibility and alertness -- So be it as ye are prepared to receive --

Ye shall now be as one prepared for the next part - and it shall be as none other - for ye shall go into fields afar and ye shall soar as the eagle - and ye shall bring back the memory of thy sojourn - - and ye shall be as one prepared to do that which I give unto thee to do -- I shall lead thee safely and surely - - fear not - for I am with thee -- So be it and Selah --

Recorded by Sister Thedra

= Acceptance =

Sori Sori -- Let that which I say be recorded for them which have the mind or will to follow where I go -- This is mine word unto them - and they shall neither add unto - or take away - they shall be as ones mindful of mine Counsel - for I have given unto them such counsel that shall profit them --

Wherein is it said that they shall obey the law -- The Word is given unto them that they be lifted up -- So be it they shall accept it in the Name of the Father - and the Son which I Am --

They shall be as ones blest of the Father - and the Light which I Am. They shall be as ones which have received the Word unto themselves, they shall take it unto themself - and be as ones blest --

Then - I shall touch them and they shall know that they have been touched -- They shall commune with me - and then they shall give unto me ear - and they shall be as ones prepared to accept me as I Am --

There are ones which claim to know me - yet they have not heard mine Voice - neither have they accepted the Word -- There are ones which are the hands and feet of me made manifest - which do mine work - mine part - which is the part that I have given unto them - - these are mine "Servants"- for they serve me - even as I serve Mine Father which hast Sent Me --

So be it that I am mindful of these Mine Servants - for it is needful that I am mindful of them -- I give unto them that which is needful - that which serves well the Great and Divine Plan --

THEY ARE AS MINE HAND & FOOT - therefore I have need of them - - it is necessary that I be watchful and mindful of them - - I say: They are never alone --

While they go and come within the "Shadows" as ones unknowing they walk with surety - they fear not - neither do they ask the rewards of men - they follow willingly and joyfully -- They ask not self-reward, Glory - nor do they fear any man's scorn -- They are as ones prepared to go where I lead them - for they know that I Am with them --

They seek the Light - they are as ones led into the Light - - they are the ones blest of the Light which I Am. They bring unto me themselves.

They ask of no man aught -- They weary not of their trials - their part -They do that which I give unto them with a glad heart - and with joy - they give unto the Father Solen Aum Solen all the Praise and the Glory.

Wherein is it said that none come unprepared - - for these are as the ones which have <u>not</u> prepared to enter into mine place of abode --

Hast it not been said: "As ye prepare thyself - SO SHALL YE RECEIVE" -- Yet they <u>think</u> I speak foolish repetitions! It is not so - for I am not given unto foolishness or idle sayings --

I am the Counselor of Counselors - - I am come that they might be <u>sobered</u>! - - that they might know that I Am about MINE FATHER'S BUSINESS! So be it and Selah --

When they are sobered - and are of the metal which I can accept into mine place of abode - then I shall do mine part -- Yet I say: I am not deceived by their flowery speech - their ceremony - creeds - customs - by the color of their skin - their honeyed words of praise - - neither am I blind unto their vain repetitions -- I am aware of that which they do - that which they say - that which they ARE! they deceive me not -- So be it I am the Light of the WORLD -- Be ye as one on whose head I place mine hand and I shall bless thee with Mine Being -- So be it and Selah --

Recorded by Sister Thedra

= God's Word =

Sori Sori --

Be ye as the hand of me made manifest unto them - and record this mine Word - that they might know that which I say unto thee --

Ye shall go into the place wherein there are ones prepared to receive thee - and ye shall give unto them as I have given unto thee -- Ye shall be as the lamp unto their feet -- and ye shall go unto them even as I have come unto thee - - for this have I prepared thee -- So be it and Selah --

Now ye shall be as one qualified - one prepared - and ye shall not fail - for I shall be with thee every step of the way - - I shall sustain thee and ye shall be glad for thy preparation -- So be it and Selah - - this is my word unto thee --

Now I shall speak unto them which ask for Light: Ye shall be blest to receive of this one which I have prepared - for she hast been as one true unto herself - as one tried - tested - and proven trust worth --

Now she shall go forth as one prepared to assist thee - - for this have I placed mine Seal upon her - and I have given unto her the "WORD" - and she shall use it for the Good of All mankind -- So be it and Selah - This shall be unto thee mine Word - and it shall not be made void - for no man shall say me NAY -- I have spoken and so shall it be - for I am He which is come that there be Light -- So let it be -- I Am that I Am

Recorded by Sister Thedra

Mission Statement

Give the truth to the world. Let it be received where it will. Many will read the messages. Some will accept the truth, others will read through curiosity, a few will ridicule. Yet to all is the truth given, and to all remains the power of choice.

The hope of the world in these times is in spiritualizing all forms of activity---promoting understanding through love and service. These must be the watchwords if the world is to come into lasting peace. We are trying to influence a world that is going astray and could cause undreamed of suffering. We are trying to overcome the thought of materialists and to bring a spiritual outlook into the earthly life. We need the help of all on earth who can think in spiritual terms. The great battle to be fought now is between the spiritual and the material, between idealism and carnalism. You can help by spreading the word---we are asking that you help because the battle may be long and the victory far away.

Halls of Light is not allied with any sect, denomination, political entity, organization, neither endorses nor opposes any cause. There are no dues for membership. Halls of Light is self-supporting through its own voluntary contributions. Halls of Light has but one purpose: to help through encouragement and understanding...

To contact the publishers or to obtain copies of our other books, please contact us at email: goldtown11@gmail.com

Sananda's Appearance

Be ye as one which hast heard Mine Voice and responded unto it - for I speak that ye hear, and I say that which is wise and prudent.

Let it be known that 1, the Lord thy God hast spoken and bear ye witness of Me, for I have made manifest Mineself that ye might know Me - and for this wast these manifestations made.

I say that I have made Mineself manifest that ye might see Me with thine mortal eyes; that ye might bear witness of Me. Yet thine companions saw and believed not; neither did they hear, for they were selfish and unprepared - yet, did I deny them?

I say; I came that they which would might see and hear. I went and came again unto Mine own. So be it that I have found; I have given unto the found that they which know not might know; that they might come to know as thou knowest.

Yet, how many hast turned from Me and persecuted thee for Mine Word. It is said, "Woe unto them which persecute Mine servants." is it not the law which they set into motion?

Yea Mine beloved, I say they bring about their own downfall. So be it that I am a compassionate one, and I would that they know what they do. So be it they shall learn well their lessons. So let it be, for this is the mercy of God, the One which hast sent Me.

So be it. I AM The Wayshower, the Lord thy God

I AM Sananda

About the Late Sister Thedra

Since the later part of the last Century, the Kumara wisdom has begun to reemerge into the world. This process began with the late Sister Thedra, whom Jesus Christ appeared physically to while on her deathbed and spontaneously healed her of cancer while she was in the Yucatan, where she had gone to accept her fate and the will of our Lord Jesus Christ.

That is when something miraculous occurred. Jesus spoke to her saying, "My name is Esu Sananda Kumara" and then sent Thedra down to the Monastery of the Seven Rays in Peru to learn the Kumara wisdom. After five years, Thedra was told to return to the United States where she founded the Association of Sananda and Sanat Kumara at Mt. Shasta in California.

While heading this organization, Thedra channeled many messages from Sananda and taught the Kumara wisdom. He introduced himself to her by his true name, "Sananda Kumara" And it was by his command that Sister Thedra went to Peru but eventually left upon being told that her experience there was complete. She then traveled to Mt. Shasta in California and founded the Association of Sananda and Sanat Kumara. A.S.S.K.

You ask, Is There a difference between Jesus and Sananda? Our Lord's name given at birth by his Father Joseph and his beloved mother Mary was Yeshua, thus being of the house of David and the order of Yoseph, he would be called Yeshua ben Yoseph. The Roman Emperors placed the name of Jesus upon the sir name of Yeshua after the Emperor Justinian adopted Christianity as the official faith of Rome and ordered that the sacred books be compiled upon approval of a specially appointed counsel appointed by the Emperor into a recognizable and uniform work titled “The Bible”. Prior to this, there never was a Bible per se.

There existed until the time of the Emperor's edict, a selection of many Sacred texts that were employed in the Sacred Teachings, many of which were copies of what the Greeks had transposed from the original texts in the Libraries of Alexandria which were originally compiled by Alexander the Great, and were destroyed by Julius Caesar, fearing that they might prove dangerous to the rule of a Caesar, an Earthly God.

In addition, it was to keep the knowledge of Alexander's Libraries out of the hands of the Ptolemy's who were said to be descended from his bloodline. At the time, Caesar had no way of knowing that vast portions of the Library were already in the Americas, in the Great Universities of the Inca, and in possession of the Mayans.

Yeshua spent many years in the East after his ascension. The Good Sheppard, upon his appearances to the Apostles after his ascension, told them that he was going to tend to his Father’s other sheep; which meant, plainly, that he was continuing upon his sacred journey. As The Ascended One, Yeshua took to himself the name of Sananda, meaning the Christed One, and Sananda was thus embraced forevermore by the Great Solar Brotherhood. To many of you this is all new, to others it will be received as a welcome easing of the wall that has so long separated two sides of the same coin. This is being placed into the ethers and the matrix of thought at this time, as it is the time of The Great Awakening, and the Christos is already emerging into the new consciousness.

Authority to use the name of Sananda was given to Sister Thedra when Jesus, (Sananda), appeared to her in the Yucatan and cured her instantly of the cancer that had taken over her body. Further, he allowed a picture of his countenance to be taken at that time that she might realize the occurrence was more than a dream. Thedra had a large format camera called a 620 that she used to take the picture of Sananda.

Sanada's Message to her by Sister Thedra: "Sori Sori: Mine hand I have placed upon thine head, and I have given unto thee the authority to use Mine name. Give unto them the name Sananda, by which they shall know Me as the Lord thy God - the Son of God, sent that ye be made to know me, the One sent from out The Inner Temple that there be Light in the world of men. Now it is come when ones which have the will to follow Me shall come to know Me by that name which I commanded thee to give unto the world as Mine New name.

There are many that shall call upon the name of Jesus, yet they will deny the new name as they are want to do. Unto thee I give assurance that I am the One sent that there be Light in the world of men. Now let this be understood, that they that deny Mine New Name deny Me by any name. So be it I have appointed thee Mine spokesman; I've given unto thee the power and authority to speak for being that which I AM. And I say unto thee Mine child whom I have called forth and anointed thee with the Holy Spirit, thy name shall be as it is now called, Thedra, that name I spoke unto thee from out the ethers, and thou heard Me and accepted that which I gave unto thee; and wherein have I deceived thee? Wherein have I forgotten thee, or left thee alone?"

I say unto thee: "Mine hand is upon thee and I shall sustain thee and you shall come to know that which I have kept for thee. So be it that I have kept thy reward, and at no time shall it be dissipated or scattered, for it is intact. So let this Mine Word suffice them which question thee - let them question, and I shall bear witness for thee. For do I not know Mine servants from the traitors? Do I not reward Mine servants according unto their works or merits? I speak that they might know that I am mindful of Mine servants, that I am not a poor puny priest who has forgotten his servants.

"I say unto them: Mine servants shall be glorified above the crowned heads of the nations which have set themselves apart, and denied Me Mine part of Mine word for they have turned from Me in their conceit and forgetfulness. Now let this go on record as Mine Word, and I shall give unto them proof, which are of a mind to follow Me.

So be it as I have spoken and I am not finished; I shall speak again and again, and I shall rise Mine Voice against them which set foot against Mine servants, and they shall be as ones cast out. So let them ask of Me and I shall enlighten them. So be it I know whereof I speak. Be ye as ones blest to accept Me and know Me for that which I AM." On Saturday, June 13, 1992, at exactly 10.00 PM, at the age of 92, Sister Thedra made her final transition from the comfort of her own bed. When the time arrived, she simply took one small breath and slipped quietly away, without pomp or fanfare.

She left as she had lived: as a humble servant for the greater good. The messages included were given to Sister Thedra shortly before her transition. They are compiled here to give you some idea of the significance of her passing and of the expansion of the work, as she is now free of the physical limitations and the pain of the past. Her work now in the higher realms will simply be an extension of that work.

Divine Explanations

Part - I

The following explanations and definitions of terms used by Sananda (Jesus) and the various Sibors were given by Sananda through direct revelation. They are not alphabetical. These explanations should be read over and over.

\- - - - - - - - - - -

"My Beloved Sibors please give us plainly the definitions of the following words that there may be no error on our part." - Thedra.

THEMSELF? What is the explanation of your terminology of "Themself" – "themselves"?

"I (Sananda) say unto thee mine beloved, they which would be unto thee a vessel, unto thee a sibor, unto thee teacher, are as ones enlightened of the Father, enlightened of the Father for the light is in them.

They know their parts well, they have their memory, they have mastered the elements, they can do all the things which I do and they take unto "themself" no credit for they have overcome self. They are self-less. Now I say unto them: them which work with thee are the Selfless ones. They ask <u>no</u>thing for "themself." Now while this is true they are as one.

They are within the great brotherhood of the Selfless Ones - the Ones clothed in white. They are as the Royal Assembly - and each unto his own, yet each for all and all for one. Now while in thy world, they (of thy world) are selfish and they are not for the whole - they ask for self and I speak of these as the selfish ones. I speak unto them in terms which they shall come to know and therein is wisdom.

I say that they shall be responsible for "themself" and as a world of me I say they shall be responsible for their society; they "themself" have created it. Now I speak unto thee mine beloved, I say "ye shall be responsible for thyself. He shall be responsible for himself. They as a whole shall be responsible for that which they have created, while thou art responsible unto thyself for thine part - and not held accountable for theirs. Be it so."

BELEIS? "Mighty is the word and great the power thereof. I say unto thee this word carries with it the part of surrender. The word is the release of power - that which is sent forth by the one which asks of the Father His blessing. It is the surrender of the self - the complete surrender of the personal will and letting the Father's will be accomplished in all things through thee. "So be it" - it the accomplishment, the acceptance of the Father's plan."

SELAH? - "The word carries the Seal of Truth - meaning it is without error - no mistake - it is the verification of Truth - not subject to change.

SIBET? – "The Sibet is one which has offered or presented himself as a candidate for the greater learning and for the greater initiation. He comes as an empty vessel that he may be filled. So be it."

SIBOR? - "I am the Sibor of Sibors." - "The Sibor is one which has been illumined of God the Father. He has returned unto the Father purified. He has gone the Royal Road - which means he has overcome death. He has mastered the lower elements - he controls the elements. He can raise the dead - heal the sick - he can create like unto the Father for he has finished his course and won the victory and returned unto the Father the Victor. So be it."

"I am the Sibor of Sibors. I am the first born of Him which hast sent me. Sananda."

LEGIRONS? - "Beloved - I say unto thee: thy opinions and thy dogmas are not the least of these - neither thy creeds. Be it ever that these are great and heavy ones. Now let it be understood that a leg-iron is something which holds thee bound. It is something which holds thee, it keeps thee fast, wherein progress is not possible. Now that progress be made possible, ye shall cut away the legirons.

Knowest thou these bound by legirons? These are to be pitied, they drag them with them, impeding their progress - and they are as ones bound! They are not free - are they? While they serve their sentence - they are as ones bound - they are bond-men - they are bound men - men bound. Now let me say I too am a "bondsman." I came that they may be free. I say I bring unto thee the law which thou shall obey - unto the letter - then I shall give unto thee that which I have kept for thee. Be ye as one prepared for that.

PREPARATION? Now - preparation - what do you mean by "preparation?" "This my beloved is the part which they shall do - the part of preparation is: cleaning thyself of all the opinions, indoctrinations of man. The cup must be emptied. This is thy part, the becoming the '"little child" unopinionated, unscathed and unmarred with or by their doctrines, creeds and crafts. I say the child is unindoctrinated and un-opinonated and is the virgin mind – (yet it does not remain so long in this world). While the little child represents the empty cup - the empty vessel, the Virgin Spirit, it is given unto the child to be one which has come from other realms and to have been in many embodiments, many times: yet the symbol of virginity. Wherein is it said there are none innocent among thee?

WHEREIN I AM? - "Now while thou art yet within the world of men - I am within mine Father's realm, the place wherein there is no darkness, wherein ALL things are known. I say wherein ALL things are known, wherein there is No mystery.

And too - I say when thou hast attained unto thy Royal Road, when thou hast become part of the Royal Assembly, thou shall know as I - thou shall be as I - thou shall be brought into the place wherein I am, for I say unto thee this is attainment. This is the day of Attainment, the day of "becoming," the day of thy salvation. Know ye that this is Mine day - the day for which thou hast waited? I say unto thee: "This is the day of fulfillment. This is Mine Day. Mine Day is come ---"

What is meant by "ALL THE LANDS OF THE EARTH?"- "This I mean, all the lands of the Earth. I have said it, I mean it as I have said it and there is no mystery of or to it."

ALL MANKIND? "This is Mine people - Mine children - Mine flock - Mine Church - Mine brethren - Mine congregation unto whom I shall minister. By Mine own hand shall they be fed and led. These have I came to find. Are not all hu-man beings considered "Man kind"? by thine own standards. Yet all men are not of me."

WHAT DO YOU MEAN - "WILL IT SO"? - "There is power in the "WILL" and the power which they use to create their own torment and confusion is misused energy. Yet they will this - they will it so. Now when ye will to serve me ye give unto me thy undivided attention, the whole heart - thy heart - thine ALL. Yet I say that they which doth attempt to serve me with one hand and the dragon with the other has not willed to serve me. They are not of me - they are not of Mine flock. I say they are either with me or against me. I cannot accept the one hand while they reserve the other for the dragon. They are not wholeheartedly mine.

I make no compromises with the dragon. Mine shall come out from them and surrender unto me themself - their all - without reservation. This is willing it so - for they will the Father's will be done in them, through them, by them. They leave no energy that the dragon may use. They use all their energy to serve me. This is mine word unto thee."

WHAT IS DARKNESS? - "Thine Un-Knowing - thy darkness comes from the fall of man - which one was with God the Father perfect which didst have his memory blanked from him when he didst transgress."

MAYAS VEIL? - "The result of such unknowing - the darkness which man has brought upon himself. The part he has created for himself."

WHAT DOES IT MEAN TO BETRAY ONES SELF? - "This is the sad part for first the 'fall' came from his betrayal - and it hast resulted in the fall - in the veil of Maya - the "illusion" and in thy un-knowing - in thy own darkness."

WHAT OF BETRAYING "HIS OWN TRUST"? - "The plan is all inclusive and includes all - yet there are ones unaware of the "plan" - (and they are not as included in this temple as yet) - no personal reference unto the ones within this temple. Now when one becomes aware of his part, he is given the law and it is provided for his own good and he has the law clearly stated, plainly recorded, and he turns his face away - that he may hide from it. He puts his fingers into his ears that he may not hear it. He gives unto his benefactors the bitter cup and he goes his own willful way.

He has betrayed himself for he shall be caught up short of his course. When he has been given a chance - a "part" within the plan and he has committed himself, he has the responsibility given unto him for that "part" and should he be so foolish as to betray his trust he shall be like unto one which has thrown overboard his own life belt - poor foolish ones!"

WISDOM? - What is meant by the word "Wisdom?" - "Wisdom is that which is light, the knowledge of the law and its proper use. The right use of the law - and this Mine children is Mine part. I come that ye may BECOME wise! Wisdom is thy divine gift - not of man, for man of Earth is foolish indeed - and he is nothing save that which the Father has endowed him. All else is of the world of "illusion" which shall pass into nothingness in the Light which I Am."

WHAT IS THE "PEARL OF GREAT PRICE, THE PRICELESS PEARL? - "That which I offer thee - thy freedom, thy salvation from bondage - thine inheritance in full - Mine word which is not purchased with coin - not bought, neither is it sold. It is the wisdom of which I speak. Mine offer unto thee is without price - it is the 'pearl' - "Mine Pearl."

WHY ARE MIS-SPELLED AND GRAMMATICAL ERRORS USED IN THESE SCRIPTS? - "I am not a conformist. I am not concerned with the letters of man for I am He which has come that they be unbound by their fetters. I say unto them which desireth the letter - unto them the letter.

I say unto thee: be ye as ones free from such bondage. I stand ready to free thee from thy bondage. Unto thee I say - give unto the letter no thought. Hear what I say for I shall say it in many ways as becomes me and serves mine purpose. I say I am no stranger in thine midst. While they know me not, I know them. I see them bowing down before the Golden Calf - and they worship at the shrines which they have set up. (Their own standards of education.) They guild them and bring unto them burnt offerings - yet they close me out.

Be ye not so foolish. Be ye not so foolish! I am come that ye might have Light - Wisdom - Freedom which is the Father's will. While the letter changeth and passeth away - and the letter is not the law - the letter is of no consequence other than to cause thee to see the "Word." The word is the power which shall provoke thine mind into action and thy mind shall be free from the letter. See what is meant within the Word, and let thine mind be staid on me - the Light, the Way - Truth and Wisdom."

"I am He which hast come - that ye be free: forever free. I am Sananda - Son of God. Once known as the Nazarine, He which was born of Mary, Ward of Joseph.

Recorded by Thedra

Part - 2

THE WHITE BROTHERHOOD AND THE EMERALD CROSS.

THE MANY QUESTIONS ABOUT THE WHITE BROTHERHOOD AND THE ORDER OF THE EMERALD CROSS MAY BE EXPLAINED IN A FEW SIMPLE WORDS.

ONE HAS TO EARN THE RIGHT TO BECOME A MEMBER - EITHER IN THIS LIFE OR OTHERS BEFORE OR AFTER - NONE ENTER UNPREPARED.

THE WHITE BROTHERHOOD - or - THE ROYAL ASSEMBLY is of the Realms of Light---not of Earth. The Ascended Masters have proven themself in the school of Earth (THE SCHOOL FOR GODS) who have trodden the path of INITIATION - overcome the trials and temptations of the mundane world - who have gained their freedom and ascended as the Lord Jesus Christ (Sananda). They have gone the ROYAL ROAD.

Knowing the path of the Initiate -- and its pitfalls -- and sorrow, they extend a hand in Fellowship - LOVE and WISDOM - NEVER depriving the candidate an opportunity to learn his lessons well -- for this is His salvation -- for this do they proffer their hand, NOT to do our part for us, but rather that we become strong and free by our own strength.

The Royal Assembly or the White Brotherhood have known all of the heartaches, the longing, crucifications, temptations and JOYS of the aspirant -- the candidate -- the Master -- the Sibor -- herein lies their strength, their understanding, their great love for us on the path.

Their love and understanding knows no bounds. They give help when necessary for our progress. They also withhold it wisely - should it deprive us of our lessons. The candidate on the path of initiation shall become self-responsible for all his actions -- all the energy allotted him throughout his whole EARTHLY existence - and make atonement for all his misused energy, for therein is his salvation.

There is no one else which will ever make this atonement for us (the candidate) on the path of unfoldment. While the host of "WHITE BROTHERS" Brothers of LIGHT are ready to assist, the candidate shall (MUST) put forth every effort to overcome all the forces of darkness which would deter his progress and earn for himself his freedom from BONDAGE.

THE EMERALD CROSS

THE EMERALD CROSS is a company – and an order of beings who work within the Brotherhood of MAN - and the Fatherhood of God - for the good of all mankind --- And at the head of this group is one known as MOTHER SARAH, the personification of love -- embodiment of all MOTHERS. That is: the LOVE of God made Manifest - in MOTHERS. The blessed Mother Sarah is the head of this Order of the Emerald Cross. And when one earns the Divine right and privileges to associate themself with this Order, it is the joy of all the Orders - and Brothers of Light. I speak for the Order - for I am known as Merseda. (As told to Sister Thedra of the Order of the Emerald Cross).

COMANCHE - which is the porter at the door - which doth keep out the unworthy, the unjust, the unclean. The Door Keeper - the one responsible for the Temple Gate.

BITTER CUP - that which you would not like to partake of - that which poisons thee, that which is not good, that which torments thee - that which ye have given unto thy brother to torment him which returns unto thee as a boomerang to torment thee - which ye shall receive multiplied - which has accumulated in its swift flight. I say prepare not for thyself the bitter cup for ye shall drink of the portion which thou doth prepare for thy brother. Be ye not foolish - make it not bitter.

BLEST OF MINE BEING - I have given of Mine self that Mine beloved has being.

BLEST OF MINE PRESENCE - Have I not gone the long way? I have gone out from Mine place of abode that I might bring light unto the Earth that she might be lifted up - that the children thereof might be delivered of all bondage - that they might return unto the place from whence they went out. And have I not come unto thee many times that this be accomplished? Have I not done all which has been given unto me to do? Wherein have I failed thee? Have I not done all that I have come to do? - While it is not as yet finished, I shall not fail. My mission shall be finished ere I return unto Mine abiding place. Shall I not be unto the true and shall I not return the Victor?

GAVE OF HIMSELF - Did I not give of Mine Self - hast thou? Have I not been true unto Mine trust? Have I asked aught for Myself? Have I not done that which I have promised? Have I not given Mine All? Have I not come on a Sacrificial Mission? What more have I to give - other than myself?

PORE - The physical body - vehicle which thou dost use.

INITIATION - Thy preparation for the inner temple. Each step is an initiation. One step at a time - the overcoming of self - the world - the becoming that which I am.

COSMOS - That which is unseen throughout many universes by thy eyes. Great is the expanse of the Father's Kingdom and the total thereof is referred to as "throughout the Cosmos."

LORD'S STRANGE ACT - This I shall reveal in Mine own time.

WALK WHICH WAY THY CROWN TILTS NOT - as a Son of God. Do honor unto thy Father Mother God - and thou shall be as one which has the Royal Raiment upon thine shoulders - and ye shall wear it in honor and with dignity.

WHEN IT SAYS IT IS RECORDED - WHEREIN IS IT RECORDED? - In the secret place - in the eth - and within the inner temple - and wherein thou art are many things recorded - which I do speak of. Ye shall see these recordings when thou doth enter into the secret place of Mine abode. I say ye shall read the records wherein are written the records of all thy travels from the time ye left the Father Mother God until thine return unto him.

WHAT IS MICHAEL'S FLAMING SWORD? - "The "Sword of Truth and justice."

Recorded by Sister Thedra

Other Books by TNT Publishing

Who am I and Why Am I here?

The Significance of Existence

Death and the Incredible Life After

Fear of Death Removed

Paradise Regained

Spiritual Laws Revealed

Unseen Forces

Too Good to Be True

The Truth of Life in the Spirit World

He Who Has Ears

The Great Awakening, Volumes I thru VII

The Great Awakening, Volume VIII,
THE WHITE STAR OF THE EAST

The Great Awakening, Volume IX,
I THE LORD GOD SAY UNTO THEM

The Great Awakening, Volume X,
MINE INTERCOM MESSAGES FROM THE REALMS OF LIGHT

The Great Awakening, Volume XI,
THE BOOK OF THE LORD

The Great Awakening, Volume XII thru XV,
TEMPLE TEACHINGS FROM THE HIGHER REALMS

Transfiguration Volumes I thru Volume VIII

Contact us at

Email: goldtown11@gmail.com

Web: https://www.whoamiandwhyamihere.com/order-online